Love in a Time of Hate

L K SHARMA

A LOVE SONG IS SUNG AGAIN!

A century has gone since the appearance of J. Alfred Prufrock. No war has undone many but in India, a socio-political crisis is ruining lives. K. Anand Kak shows that regardless of time and distance, human impulses remain the same. Kak wants to be loved. He suffers from the Prufrock Syndrome, highlighted by T. S. Eliot, that decades later got identified by modern medicine as alexithymia.

factionbooks@gmail.com

CRITICS SAY

"Unabashedly romantic, the poem manages to capture so much of infatuation without ever veering into the maudlin, maintaining a certain ironic self-awareness. Will-they-won't-they aspect of the romance provides a suspenseful counterpoint to the serious political content. The story structure, which through various foreshadowing elements keeps us guessing whether the narrator will achieve his goal, does a really good job of keeping the suspense up as we move through the various political and philosophical themes and tonal variations."

"The poem portrays Love in the time of quarantine in an India transformed into a weird nation by a political adventurer."

"Serious political analysis is beautifully woven in with a love story, illustrating how the nature of a regime affects individual mental health and personal relationships."

"I especially enjoyed the Hinglish section. But the patterns and verve of spoken conversation are throughout the book, most seamlessly laced with the rhythm and flow of poetry."

"A glimpse of what technological advances are doing to love."

"The number of literary citations that the poet manages to fit in is quite staggering. I surprised myself at how many I caught, although I'm sure a whole bunch slipped past me as well."

Lonely *Romantic* REALIST

Conflicted INADEQUATE Unsure

FAILURE Inhibition FANTASY

Aging **Fear** [illegible] **self-doubt**

Isolation alienation IDENTITY

LOVE IN INDIA TODAY

K. Anand Kak describes his tryst with a 21st century woman. Kak's monologue reveals his inner life and his relationship with an activist-poet. Kak faces Prufrock's Predicament. Like J. Alfred Prufrock, he is diffident and shy of women. He feels lonely, fears failure, and doubts his sexual identity. Kak's woman, unlike Prufrock's, is not a silent and shadowy creature. He portrays her. She shares with Kak her despair over India's tragic state. She protests all the time against hatred, bigotry and mendacity fuelled by a populist leader who wins power by polarising people and turbo-charging their worst instincts. She writes political poems, lamenting the end of the idea of India. Kak has to compete with a nation to get her attention! Every night, she rejects his cowardly erotic moves and he retreats quietly. One night, while they are in her room, a rare event occurs. Kak's dream is realised. He escapes Prufrock's fate. But a single night does not fulfill his life. What next, Kak wonders.

T. S. Eliot gave me life.

With his visions, indecisions, and revisions, shaped me as quintessentially Eliotic.

KAK'S INHERITANCE

K. Anand Kak's lineage is brilliantly illustrated by Julian Peters in his book on *The Love Song of J. Alfred Prufrock*. Eliot uses words, while Peters uses brush to portray the immortal lover. Bombay-based K. Anand Kak inspires Peters to place Prufrock in India. So, on the book cover, Prufrock is seen walking towards the flat of his love interest, casting yearnful eyes on a couple enjoying on the Marine Drive in Bombay. Peter's illustrations set the scene for Anand Kak's monologue of love and despair.

BY T.S. ELIOT ILLUSTRATED BY JULIAN PETERS

LET US GO, THROUGH CERTAIN HALF-DESERTED STREETS,

AND SAWDUST RESTAURANTS WITH OYSTER SHELLS:

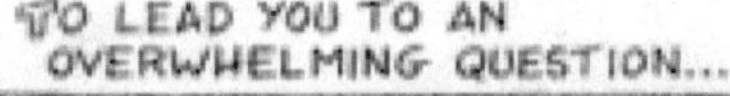
TO LEAD YOU TO AN OVERWHELMING QUESTION...

IN A MINUTE THERE IS TIME
FOR DECISIONS AND REVISIONS
WHICH A MINUTE WILL REVERSE.

THERE WILL BE TIME TO WONDER,

AND,

TIME TO TURN BACK AND DESCEND THE STAIR,

TO PREPARE A FACE
TO MEET THE FACES
THAT YOU MEET;

THE EYES THAT FIX YOU

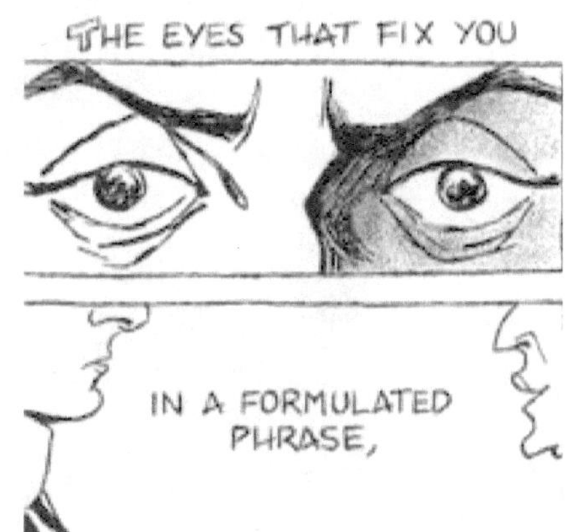

WITH A BALD SPOT
IN THE MIDDLE OF MY HAIR

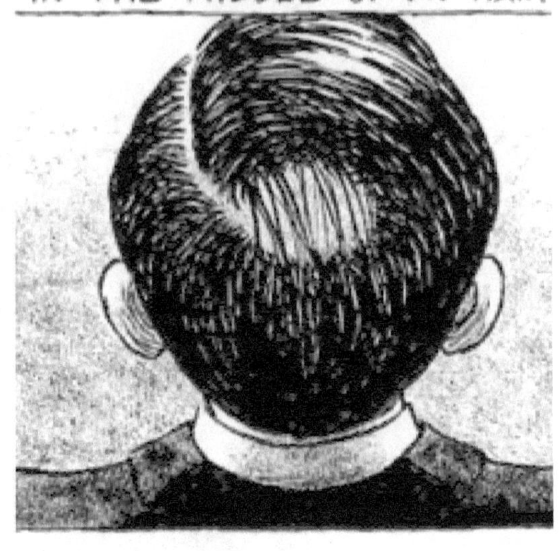

SHALL I PART MY HAIR BEHIND?

I GROW OLD...

I SHALL
WEAR THE
BOTTOMS OF
MY TROUSERS
ROLLED.

IS IT PERFUME FROM A DRESS
THAT MAKES ME SO DIGRESS?

DO I DARE TO EAT A PEACH?

CONTENTS

I

Night after Night

Tonight, you open your dark door,
looking radiant, smiling that smile.
Tagore makes me say: The light on
your face is *His Light.*

Marlowe lends me the line
"Come live with me..."
Singers who split live and love
beam their voices into my head.

I borrow words from Auden and
feel like telling you that we must
love each other or die.

We are face to face. My feeling for
you rages on. Recognised by this
room, dark theatres, dim-lit cafes,
sunlit parks, crowded shops and
deserted streets. All have seen my
eyes gazing at you.

We begin in a contrived corridor
to continue in your room. Read
Eliot, share silences and solitude
to show solidarity of the solitary.

An overwhelming question reaches
my tongue. Are you thinking what
I am thinking? I do not drop it in
your plate.

You don't ask me whether I am happy
to see you or is it something in your
pocket? You might ask me one day.

In Landor's words, I say you smile,
you speak, and I believe. Does every
word or smile deceive? Like Landor,
I want you to deceive and deceive me
again!

Your lips part only to talk. Invite me
to talk. Why is it so? What do I do?

Put on some weight. Hide my skinny
arms, spindly legs, and balding head.

You explore and excite my mind.
Your mind moves. How do I
move your body to touch mine?
Do I quote Larkin to entice you
with the four-letter word widely
popularised by the poet among
the genteel women of England?

Shall I recite a *nazm* to say the
unsayable? A heroine sings one
to signal come-hither. She hints,
unlike her western counterpart
who screams: *Come, dirty me*!

Shall I acclaim your beauty or sing
of your cruelty? Vow to love for
ever with oaths and hyperboles.
Repeat the mantra that the moon
and stars will disappear but I shall
be with you, life after life!

You never nod. How do I make any
headway? Days go by. Nights go by.
We go nowhere.

Your poem *Love in a Time of Crisis*
ignores my love that is in a crisis!
Not that words will satiate me.

I am here every night. You come so
near, remain so far. Am I cursed
like Tantalus? How long will I have
to live like him?

Our love lay dormant in the cruellest
winter month. Will our love-life
bloom this spring? Will your room
turn into our bedroom for one night?
I can do nothing but hope.

II

Abandon Your Cause

How will we get to meet, unless you
end your obsession with the nation.
You live with India, day, and night.
Possessed by the idea of India.

You tell me where India is going. You
take me through the day's depressing
developments. I want to take you in a
rose garden. I talk of us; you talk of
India. I am up against a country.

Your heart beats for a cause, not for me.
Your views about India are very strong,
feeling for me very weak. You feel

anguished about the nation and want
me to feel the same.

You like me. Want to see me every night.
I come without fail. You welcome me
but cannot make up your mind as to how
far should you go! You switch TV
channels,
doom-scroll, and chat about the Leader's
irresistible rise and unlikely fall. You
never strike a chirpy note. Our nights
are laden with words and gloom.

You talk of India, its ills and descent
into hell. You say this is not the India
you had seen or dreamt of. India is
regressing. Going back to the medieval
age. New India is mythological India.
You fear a new Mahabharat, a grand
battle within the family.

Masses are fed imagined history and
myths by millions of hired internet
nutters. There is an astounding rise
of unreason. Non-issues dominate
faux debates that publicise hate
merchants, opening and scratching
healed wounds.

The past is virulent for a nation as for an individual. The Leader invokes the past. His army fights over memory and seeks to avenge a Mughal emperor's bigotry by indulging in bigotry. It ignores the depredation by the British rulers.

His vigilantes invoke patriotism to drain away knowledge from society and damage universities, centres of liberal democracy. The deafening chants of nationalism drown the cries of injustice, poverty and protests against the Government's misadventures and dismal performance.

Welcome to the Mumbo Jumbo Nation. March of modernity stopped. Progress nullified. Intellect and scientific temper derided. Dissent suppressed. Dissenters silenced. The concept of truth obliterated.

The idea of India destroyed. Mendacity rules. Paranoia and mistrust envelope us in this communal cauldron bubbling with hatred. Built by freedom-fighters, India is being demolished by those who had kept away from the freedom struggle.

Churchill had forecast who will rule independent India. Some Indians too feared that India was not ready for universal franchise. India got too much democracy too early. They say had Britain been a democracy in the time of Robin Hood, that outlaw would have been the Prime Minister!

For long independent India was ruled by those who and whose fathers had fought for freedom and gone to British jails. These liberals ignored the threat of sectarianism. Communal leaders took advantage of the liberal ethos and spread their tentacles to destroy secular ethos and promote their version of Hinduism.

The Hindu right-wing had failed to grab power so long as Indians remembered the tragedy caused by religious extremism and polarisation. The fanatics waited in the wings, knowing that human memory is short.

India's secular fabric developed holes, giving an opportunity to leaders using cadres to oppress a minority and incite the majority by making it feel besieged. They fight the faith of a frightened minority and fragment society.

They proved that liberal democracy was fragile and could be pushed on the path of terminal retreat. We had taken the idea of India for granted. The bubble in which the liberals lived was small and got punctured easily.

In the Republic of Fear, children are groomed to be vigilantes. The power of rumour to destroy dissenters and institutions and create an ugly society is established. Mass consciousness is poisoned.

Language has been distorted. Words given new meanings. Insidious and invidious confront us. Mobs march waving flags as sticks. Menace the Other, lynch the nation.

We are at war, struck by weapons of mass disinformation. Suffocated by smoke of the digital battlefield. No decaying corpses. Decaying women and men stare and cry, seeking safety from deafening digital shelling.

An ancient faith hijacked and turned into a political weapon. Hindu saints watched it all. Said nothing to defend

their faith and explain true Hinduism
to those claiming to follow this noble
faith.

You say religious right-wingers and
fake nationalists are ruining India.
Secularism buried under 20 million
paid tweets. People's courts punish
those promoting inter-faith harmony.

As to the Gandhian legacy, an MP
applauds Gandhi's assassin. A woman
in saffron robes enacts the murder of
the Mahatma and praises his killer.

She is hailed by her saffron-dressed
followers. Her video showing a pistol
and flowing blood is liked by many.
Some pray at the Godse Temple!

Such weird scenes are to be seen to
be believed. Video wars are fought
with viral lies and fake news.

Indians now live in Absurdistan.
It has become the new normal.
The Deep State watches and rules.

Fear stalks the infantilized nation.
Officials fall in line. As per orders,

they wreck vengeance on the innocent to settle scores with the critics of the Leader. Those asked to commit crimes for political gains are fully protected and allowed to go scot free.

Business leaders and Bollywood stars turned out to be men of low character. Big A B or C shake their hips in public and shake with fear in private. They seal their lips and look the other way when their few fearless colleagues are trolled by vigilantes and threatened by the despotic Government.

M*aha Nayaks* masquerade as heroes, fight the reel villains and sell snake oil for a fee. Filmmakers make films to please the Leader.

Order vanished. Laws redundant. Judges know which side their bread is buttered. Politicized police have been given a new charter of duty. State-sponsored vigilantes wield the weapon of religion. They have tasted blood. Private armies march through the night.

Conspiracism has won. Manipulation
is the key to power. We cannot think.
We are drugged. Drunk on hate, we
laugh and kill, kill, and laugh and
indulge in mass hysteria.

The itch to be violent has gone virulent.
A riot is engineered at a moment's
notice. Green fields become killing fields
when visited by women in the morning.

At night, the TV studios become boxing
arenas. The power-drunk anchor jumps
up and down shrieking, striking hands
in the air, demanding drugs, to launch
a million tweets praising his ugly show.

Bear-baiting and public executions gone
out of fashion. Humans enjoy dogfights
among humans. They watch the idiot box
and enrich the channels that spread hate.

Clowns play politicians. Politicians clown.
They fool and amuse to win poll after
poll.
Their failure of intent has caused a
disaster.
All-consuming polarisation has destroyed
social harmony as well as internal
security.

The crapification of the Indian mind is beyond treatment. A novelist needling politicians with her luminous prose, is derided as activist-writer. Let us be hyphenated at the hips!

Poets and politicians are drawn to the power of words. Poets use these to express, wonder and find answers. Politicians use these to beguile and mobilise people. Poets say what others cannot or do not.

Some say poetry is a luxury enjoyed by the educated middle classes and schools should not teach poetry because it is irrelevant. "Poetry, though heavenly born, consorts with poverty and scorn". Poetry makes nothing happen! A poet says so. You say no. Poetry makes things happen, things that are not seen.

Poetry makes you live, helps you cope with sorrow. It provides a healing touch. It is way of trying to come to peace with the world. This "charming nymph is neglected and decried". What is worse, studied as text. You believe "the blood jet is poetry and there is no stopping it."

As a poet, you sense what is coming
long before it does, as animals sense
a tsunami or an earthquake. So, you
know where India is headed.

A culture war precedes a religious war.
It will take decades to recover what we
lost in a few years. Our civilization is
losing its resilience. The genie is out. It
can't be pushed back into the bottle.
The lie outlasts the liar. The toxic
political culture will not let a sensible
leader emerge. No one will be able
to make this country governable.

Future looks grim. Post-truth politics
has ushered in a pre-fascism phase.
and fascism has had a good trial run.

You call India Prozac Nation and get
away with it since semi-literate
nationalists think it is a compliment.

India turned upside down. Bigotry,
misogyny, sectarianism, hatred and
violence have become all pervasive.

You believe protest poems will make
a difference, change the world. Words

are weapons but the Pope has few
battalions and the Leader knows it.

Writers have been maligned and
marginalized. Logicians have
no role. A semiotician in India has to
look both sides before crossing a road.
A philosopher bolts back on seeing a
mob on the street.

Intellectuals who alert the nation
have been rendered toothless. In
future, books will appear with titles
such as *Not So Strange Death
of the Liberal India.*

Conflict has paid a rich political
dividend. Those who engineered
a moral panic will keep the conflict
running in order to demonise the
Other. The people do not flock to
a Messiah during peaceful, normal
times. Perennial conflict is needed
to keep the Leader in power.

You are not a born poet. This cruel,
violent, divided, and fearful nation
turned you into a poet. You enrich
your poems with politics. I see you
writing *Notes from a Dead Nation.*

You see evil. Recite *Second Coming.*
"*Things fall apart; the centre cannot*
hold. The best lack all conviction while
the worst are full of passionate intensity."

Things have indeed fallen apart.
The beast that was to come,
arrived and we welcomed it!

Your protest poems, infused with
lyrical anguish, boil with rage.
Political is personal and personal
is political. I say the same to those
asking me not to take it personally
and not let my blood boil.

You light a candle, but no light can
dispel this darkness. That Yellow Fog
was benign. The mental fog is dense.
All have been hit by organised rage.
You and I remain on the same page.

Contrary to the mantra recited often,
our sacred *Janani Janmabhoomi,*
the motherland, is no Heaven. It has
turned into Hell that many of its sons
leave and many more want to leave.

Please abandon your cause. Shift your
focus from national affairs to our affair.

III

Forget Him, Think of Me

In this darkness, you talk of the
Divider-in-Chief who injects a daily
dose of hateful rhetoric, raising fear
and insecurity. As a teller of lies and
super-spreader of hate, he competes
with Trump, you say.

He sells hyper-nationalism that fuels
bigotry, hatred, and violence. Comes
from the same state that produced
the Great Unifier. Ironic!

He imitates Vivekanand and Tagore
with make-up and sartorial props.
His stylist will get a national award.

He shows off hyper-masculinity, like the British rulers who got themselves photographed with a dead tiger under their feet. He boasts of his chest size and carries on his decivilizing mission.

Efforts to legislate minds and control thought have succeeded. While the crude barriers to the movement of protestors are seen by the world, the ban on the movement of ideas gets less attention.

Voters like his display of masculinity and posturing. They go sleepwalking to the polling booths under the influence the witches' brew of fear and hope. We get the leaders we get.

The finely attired Leader struts on the world stage. Builds tall iron and stone pillars of identity and turns them into sites for exhibition of nationalism and tourism. He wants to be remembered through grand monuments.

A mass psychologist, who interviewed the Leader several years ago, said he had met a text-book fascist. Scholars are not read. So, the Leader climbed the power ladder and rose to the top, fulfilling his life's ambition.

The academic later warned that one entire generation of Indians will have to pay the price for the havoc being caused by the political adventure kick-started through polarisation.

Moderation and restraint are banished from discourse. Patience for nuance is lost. Hope is derived from rumours.

Scholars calculate the human costs of tragic transformation that historians will record years from now. Books will appear on the descent of the nation and the spell of mass hysteria that enfeebled India and Indians.

The scholar who alerted the nation has met Indians to whom India feels like a foreign country. Constant social strife is ruining their mental health. Their pain is proportionate to the elation felt by the vigilantes going after their victims.

You say the Leader intensifies our anxieties and weaponises these against us. A health expert says the endemic

continuous traumatic stress will cause
a mental health crisis. Fear aggravates
the malady.

GDP-obsessed economists pooh-pooh
the idea of the Gross National Happiness.
Some political scientists dare to say that
democracy cannot survive the loss of a
sense of identity and purpose.

Any internal security expert will say
that powerlessness increases depression
and makes people more vulnerable
to extremism.

Psephologists write on two narratives
going on in this divided nation, one
backed by populism, rhetoric, lies and
state power. The other backed by facts
and reason, rendered ineffective by a
vicious campaign against "intellectuals".

The talented Leader manipulates mass
behaviour. Through dramatic gestures
and words, he makes people angry or
ecstatic, as per his requirement of the
moment. A blatant persuader. He has
gauged our stupidity and pliability.

He may not have gone to a university but understands mass psychology and India's religious and social fault lines better than academics. He thinks big and has global ambitions. The religious card has got him a large following of long-distant nationalists and the Hollywood Hindus.

The Leader is a 21st century man even though he learnt to wear trousers late. His wardrobe is the envy of film stars. He owned a digital camera before it was invented and knows all about camera angles. His mentor calls him the best event manager.

He understands data science better than any IITian. He is smarter than an algorithm in tracking our hopes and fears. The toolkit containing the two lets him control the hearts and minds as he plays the right notes.

His ability to invent false narratives makes him a literary genius. He tells tales to conquer the soul of the nation. Just as the British did with stories of their supposed sense of justice and fair play!

He uses simple messages to bewitch simple people. Rhymes to entertain the masses. Uses innuendo to say the unsayable. Delivers his message without risking legal action. He commands and controls social media that gets users addicted to lies.

In conjuring up enemies of the nation, he gave lessons to Trump. He demonizes the Other and reaps political dividends. Unleashes divisive politics, branding half the people as enemies. Polarisation divides all but pays him richly.

He came to power by appealing to the worst instincts of voters and expands his empire by turbocharging these. The bigots feel empowered to act.

The mantra of *beg, borrow and steal* lets him enlarge his constituency. He wins some opponents by offering pelf and power and some by threatening to fix them. He says in public: “I have everyone’s birth-chart”, which forces others to flock to him out of fear. Once in his party, their crimes are forgotten.

You say he seduced India by envy and hate and pushed it into the infamous company of failing democracies.

Corralled a corrupt populace, lapdog media and obliging oligarchs who keep him aloft. He returns the favour and enriches his selected cronies.

The Leader parrots the Sanskrit saying "the world is one family" but makes each community see itself as different from the Other and the Other as the Other.

He makes us believe the world is illusory. Nothing is as shown, and everything is the opposite of what we are told. He convinces the multitude that facts are fiction and lies are truthful.

Ignorance is a virtue. Deception is state policy. We have entered the Age of Humbug and Hypocrisy. A smart operator propped up by bots rules our *Andher Nagri.*

You say the Leader is lucky since the
Big Power has turned Islamophobic.
It is no longer keen to destabilise
India which it used to be during the
times of Nehru and Indira. The Big
Power now sees India as an ally and
and appreciates the Leader for his
majoritarianism.

The Western press used to take the
cue from America, run down India
and never report its achievements.
It turned friendly when American
foreign policy changed and the US
corporations began to see India as
an opportunity.

Democracy is dead. Leader is elected
again and again in mobocracy.
A demagogue kills democracy with
ease starving it of secularism.

Communal hatred keeps him in power.
Capitalists nourish him. Eminent persons
want to enjoy his patronage. The poor
hope he will give the promised gifts.
The megalomaniac's writ runs and runs.

Tragedies will be written on repression
used to control distress when the Leader

failed to manufacture consent. Studies
will appear on the dangerous power
of crowds and mass emotions.

These will explain the outbreak of
tribalism and analyse how and why
people came under great pressure to
take political sides and see things in
terms of black and white.

* * *

You are right. I repeat your words
to convince you that I am with you.
But I must alert you. Don't talk
about him. Never sing songs
against him or for democracy.
Erase from your mind the words
freedom and civil liberties.

Do not think. Thinking is banned for
reasons of national security. And even
after you stop thinking, be vigilant.
You will be damned because of your
region, religion, caste, or diet.

Don't phone any friend to express
anger about the wretched state of
the nation. Walls have ears. Walls

have eyes to read your thoughts and
transmitters to that send your sound
bytes to the Agency.

Beware! The IT Cell is watching you.
It has listed you as an anti-national
involved in an international conspiracy
to spread rumors of rapes to defame
India. It magnifies the demand that you
leave India and go away to Pakistan.
You are vulnerable, not being one of
His Maidens who hailed Him and
secured rewards and personal safety.

India is no place for you. Your poems
have attracted the attention of the cyber
goons. You cannot escape the clutches
of the ghoulish machine of the IT Cell.

My messages to you will be published
to portray you as a fallen woman.
Pouted lips on photoshopped face will
go viral projecting you as a pouncing
vixen.

Your photos will be morphed to retail
your "ignoble" past. This is the least
you must expect, if not an attack on
the street or raids by official agencies.

They have finished Gauri Lankesh
and other rationalists. India is no
place for non-believers. If you want
to live in India must believe in Him.

You must stop shouting political
slogans in order to protect your
self and sanity. I fear for you. India
is not what it was. Nor are its police
or courts. The ruler did not need
any Constitutional provision to
impose Emergency and silence
the people. Official agencies know
his mind and go after the targets.

Bollywood and advertising industry
is held to ransom by His devotees.
You are a single woman. They will
trace you, chase you and maul you.

Literature can critique and condemn
the powerful. Not to talk of Orwell
and Auden; Shakespeare, Milton,
Wordsworth, Byron, and Shelley, all
wrote on politics. Dante even paid
for it. Shelley was not allowed to visit
India because of his political views.

* * *

Millions know who is responsible
for the state India is in. You feel
so disturbed by what he does to
India that you even use the four-letter
word that I cannot repeat before you.

I detest him for what he does to us.
He has no health warning inscribed
on his forehead. His noises ruin our
love life. He robs me of your time.

He hijacks you to the world of pain
and away from me. Because of him,
you sing no love lyric to me.

You shed tears not for me but for the
nation. But for the dreadful thoughts
about him, your lips would feel mine!

* * *

You ask me how we can keep gazing at
each other and avoid looking at India.
I do feel guilty for feeling romantic and
being in your room instead of the war
trench dug in every house where families
fight at dining tables over a politician,
the elephant in the room.

The reality of India that disturbs you will kill my romance. I live an anomalous co-existence, night after night.

Come with me and be my activist-lover! Not a common tribe. Considering what we are going through, it should be. As a lover in India of 2021, you are who you ought to be. I understand but resent it.

I get disappointed on hearing you. I share your anxiety. Try to banish all thoughts that are not about us. I think of only you. Nation is too big and abstract for me.

It is seen differently by different groups. Some see it in Gandhi's spinning wheel. Others in a postal stamp. Bigots call it Hindu Nation, cleansed of the Other.

Fanatics see it as saffron or green. Chefs call it Turmeric Nation. Real estate goons see India as a project site with forests to be cleared and ponds filled up with rubble. They see India as the next Las Vegas.

Our motto *Truth Alone Triumphs* is what India should be about but is not. Tagore warned us against nationalism.

Like Gandhi, he gets trolled by Hindu nationalists. Patriotism is the last refuge of scoundrels.

They attack the nation in the name of nation. Their nation is a map on paper, a figure of imagination that they invoke to beat the Other. They paint the nation as Goddess and masquerade as her worshippers in order to mobilise fools and win polls.

Their Mother India is fierce. She kills to protect her devotees. A film imagined a different Mother India played by Nargis who ploughed the field to nourish her family. She bears the burden with courage and fortitude. She is just and fair.

A poet sees Mother India as a poor frail woman with dry and dishevelled hair and a sad sickly face, unable to feed or protect her sons and daughters. The poet is called names by the fake nationalists.

* * *

These images do not matter. Unlike you, I am not obsessed with your nation. I try hard not to care what state India is in.

I do see the fascists and barbarians at
the gates. I repeat your sentences about
the current situation. But I focus on you.
I wish you will do the same. Live for me,
not for the nation.

There are sorrows other than India.
I have no sorrow other than love.
You are more precious than India.
What is India to me? You are
everything. My sweetheart comes
before Mother India.

They say if the nation is in such deep
distress, how do I sing a Love Song.
They should know the most famous
Love Song was published during the
War. There is a crisis now but there
was a far bigger crisis then.

Pain intensifies my love for you. Share
my pain to lessen it. Stop thinking.
Feel me all over. Here, here, and here!
I do not want an anguished citizen
wailing about the nation. I want a
woman to behold and to hold.

Recite your poem if you prefer that to
kissing me. I listen to you on our dismal

state and devious rulers. But how long will we go on doing that and not what couples on the Marine Drive do every evening?

You hear music in light and see light in music. So, surely, you must see above my spindly legs and below my balding head. I hope one night you would want more than my ears.

One night, when your mind gets tired and heart gets hot, you will shut your eyes and see me. That night, India would cease to matter. You will turn to me, touch me and grab my all.

On that blessed night, you would feel the whole of me and I would feel the real you. And on that holy night you will discover joy that you have never known in your life that remained satiated with ideas and starved of emotions.

What a real joy it will be to be going where I have been wanting to go and waiting to go.

IV

The Romantics

Like you, I lament the state we are
in. We are all engaged in a macabre
communal dance, amusing ourselves
to death amid a deafening din.

There was a time when I was young
and gay. I imagined daffodils in the
poetry class but they have all gone.
Gone because you did not say Yes.

I digress. The perfume from your dress.

How do I understand you? You are a
digital native with virtual presence.
Personal data is not adequate.

Technology reads lips, not minds and
hearts. What you feel is not what you
say. No one can say what she feels.
End of the quote. You are a poet.
Poetry confuses. It does not explain.
I depend on your face for a clue.
I wait for an intimate move that will
make explaining redundant.

A kiss does that as lovers know.
They kiss to crush thought,
inflame passion and end a fight.
We do not fight. I wait in vain.

Your latest poem is inviting. It
shows an opening but causes
cognitive dissonance. Your words
and gestures are out of sync.

I try to understand you and will
do so even if it takes a lifetime.
So, let's be together for lifetime.
Come closer and understand me.

You are preoccupied with thoughts!
You do not cease from exploration.

Am I an entity you are stuck with till
you explore life with an esoteric man

in a remote tribal village of beauty,
away from life's ugliness?

Who am I to you? A passing fad, a
convenience. A board to play and
test your words on, to get relief. I am
not your life, merely an insignificant
supplement to your life.

You are lost in literature. Nexus
between literature and love, like
that between literature and life,
is thorny. Both good and bad.

Literature inspires love but makes
it impure, less spontaneous and
second-hand. Book lovers imitate.
Borrow words and gestures.

We are products of text. At the
crucial moment, you are sure to
get distracted by an idea, some
character, the plot, or the writer's
words.

During intimate seconds, you will
recall similar moments in your pet
heroine's life or a scene from a play.
You will look for the meaning of
intercourse, not experience it.

You are obsessed with heroes. I, a
mere living man, how do I compete
with creatures crafted by masters?

Do you love to love or to discuss the
idea of love? As if to assure me, you
dig nails into the mattress, look
agitated and come closer. You start
sharing your intimate feelings. That
makes my fancy fly. Giving famishes
the craving. I crave but cannot have.

You abruptly say, 'I am not that'.
Your mind wonders *to or not to.*
You are enthralled by an ism. That
is why it is this far and no further,
which leaves me stricken with doubt.

I am metaphoric. I try to move you
with a melodramatic monologue.
I have messed up my copybook.
Hiding behind a mask, I seek to
attract you with words borrowed
or bought. How long can I fool you?

I raise questions, get no answers.
I go on and on. You have heard
it all. Do I jar and jangle you and
tangle your nerves? Will you turn

away? Why are you silent? Speak
to me. Say something, anything.

Let us go, You and I… Or shall
I say: *Come with me!* What do
you prefer? You don't know
what you desire or fear.

I have wandered farther then I
had wanted. We get along but
we are not getting on. Not
getting anywhere. Shall we call
it a day? It was too good to last.

The stream of consciousness changes
course! Why break away? Carry on
and enjoy the impermanence of the
waiting room. It is no doghouse.

Continue this journey without end,
on the eternal road, counting alternate
milestones of faith and doubt, passing
by romantic or dreadful stops.

Why not while away time, watching
our shadow play in *Maya Nagri,*
the City of Illusions. In it, I'm the
actor and the audience. On the stage
and on the seat.

Nothing lasts. All will end. If I outlast
you, what will I do? Recite the Vedas in
the morning, play Beethoven at night.
Talk nonsense to senseless people.
Make calls, send WhatsApp messages.
Reassure friends, irritate others.

Your absence may make me a poet.
A Hindi poem says: *Virahi hoga*
pehla kavi, aah se upja hoga gaan.
Torn apart from you, I will write
the saddest sweetest song.

I recite a poem. You ask me what is
poetry. The word originated from a
Greek word. Google knows it all!
You email a poem. Before I read it,
Gmail drafts my reply. It says:
"How beautiful!" Gmail misleads
me with a false positive by sending
me YES from you. The computer
interfaces with your brain but
slips. Google picks your YES only
by watching you googling Molly
Bloom saying YES.

Google puts our affair in auto-mode!
It horrifies you. It tickles me! It may
end your procrastination. Move you

forward. Bridge the gulf between
longing and attaining.

I am troubled by life and by after-life.
Where will our photos, videos and
bundles of memories go? The digital
legacy of our nightly text with the
sub-text will be read between the lines.
Vicarious pleasure will be derived.

Will we be denied? Records will
record that we happened. We shall
hover as ghosts. Sanskrit has the
same word for past and ghost.

You tease, you doubt, discuss doubt,
evade the explicit, suspend disbelief,
prevaricate, defer decisions, avoid
action, skip the known knowns.

Your finger is a on the Pause Button.
I am not sure of the next moment.
Will you always smile, wipe your dark
eyes with the white handkerchief?

Will you change in order to meet me?
Present is painful. Future looks bare.
You have elsewhere. I have nowhere.
I am stuck between Heaven and Hell.

Can't go. Not gone. Cannot go.
Not going. Hanging on in a steady
state on your terms. Where do I go?
You do not let me go, nor let me in.

I am in your room every night.
I shall be here tomorrow night.
Sitting in dim light. You and me,
huddled together, doing nothing.

I keep waiting. Waiting. Waiting
without a coin in hand. Without
limelight. Without audience.
My life reduced to three words:
Perhaps. Perhaps. Perhaps.

We are never alone. Three is a crowd.
Your India. India. India. Whatever it
was, whatever it is. It would go down
further. Its destroyers have tasted blood.
They will be more vicious and win more
victories. This battle will last long.

Let us get away from it all to live
and be merry. Let us migrate to
the land of imagination. They are
hacking everything. We hack time.
Come with me on time travel.

There was a time when... There was a time. Time present, Time past. Imagine its second coming. A palindrome of time.

Let's be in the romantic past in the age when no Dystopian fiction is written. All read only fairy tales. We meet by meadow, grove, and stream. Couples flirt, frolick, make merry, not think of the nation.

You are the heroine and I the hero! Our life has song and dance. There is no pain except the pain of parting. Alas, we can't linger on in that land of imagination and escape this evil time for long.

Why not accept us as 2021 lovers? Lovers are made not born. You would have been different in the romantic era. This age produced you as you are! I would not have liked to miss you. I love you as you are. I am all for modernity. I cannot observe tedious traditions that go against my liberal spirit.

You talk so freely of love. Why be
against lust? Let's do lust while
continuing to pine for love. Love
is needed when hearts are suffused
with hate. Hate is hyphenated with
Love. Love survives only in the Sunday
morning sermons.

Hate coming through newspapers
affects our mornings. It turns you
into a concerned citizen. While
having cups of tea, you need to
exchange anguish over the phone.
The outer world intrudes into inner
world. Its toxic fumes choke your
voice.

We meet every night but we do not
read together. You tell me what you
read. We do not cook together. We
don't sleep together. That is why my
insomnia is not known to you. Your
aches and pains not known to me.
Only in dreams are we together.

Your sacred chant of *Shivoham*,
generates an impure impulse in
me because I hear no words, only
see your moving lips. From the

sacred, I go to profane. I recite an erotic Sanskrit poem and also the *Song of Solomon.* Call me naughty. Being nice is fine but I must remain human, not turn Divine. I sin as God wants no competition. No redemption without damnation.

Intimations of mortality enhance grief but bring us closer. Still, our discourse remains dry. Lacks emotional intensity. Our inaction wastes the privacy of your room.

We find solace not in philosophy but in philology, wordplay being an artefact of shared interest. We discuss identity, self, the other, enigma, attachment, detachment, modernity, nostalgia, tradition and individual talent, willing suspension of disbelief and negative capability.

We define and redefine isolation, alienation, metaphysical, physical and such other concepts. You love words. You flirt with infatuation, affection, passion and get nowhere.

Words have no meaning. Words change as per the colour of the speaker. Word-making does not lead to world-making. You can go on playing with words.

You always get me lost in a verbal labyrinth while I want to get lost in you. Verbal acts don't take us far and not where I want us to go. Our linguistic foreplay is not an end in itself. We enact a scene but never follow it up with the act. Meeting of minds is a nice aperitif but is of no use unless followed by the main course.

Wordplay is never used as foreplay. You keep playing with words. Do they touch your heart? "It's always words that undress you", someone said. I want words to show your body. Even a Sanskrit erotic poem does not help.

Someone said poetry makes nothing happen. I do not believe it. Though in our case, nothing really happens. Our dialogue drags on.

To please you, I do highfalutin talk
while thinking of what you may call
a base act. Posing as an intellectual,
I show off creativity and poetic
anxiety, suppressing simple joviality.

I love to talk about exile. You tell
me about the plight of those exiled
within India. The Bihari taxi driver
in Bombay who sings a folk song
to remember and celebrate the *desh*
he left behind to earn livelihood and
send money home. The Bengali maid
in Bombay who has not gone home
for more than three years.

Naipaul popularised dislocation and
made exile glamourous. It is romantic
to remember the homeland from
the comfort of England and to indulge
in nostalgia in spare time.

Even in my hometown of Bombay,
I masquerade as an exilic hero.

I tinker with self, swing between
transition and modernity. I hide
behind the mask. This world has
only masks, not men.

You dislike jargon but you want to
'recover meaning'! I am losing it.
Missing the meaning of manhood.

I return to you. I do not kiss your
rosy cheeks. No Moorish wall
within our reach. You want to be
called mountain flower. I know
who inspired you.

I call you a poem. You put me in touch
with myself! You join me in my voyage
of self-discovery. Our path hits a barrier
as sensing danger, you withdraw some
steps, smile and change the topic.

I switch the channel. Read a message
in signs and a world in your words.
Imagine the next move, next time,
next place, next chat, and next date.

You signal again that you would
not let me grasp the nettle and
seize the day.

I follow you. I recompose my face
to meet your face. I get bewitched
by your beauty. A tremor hits me.
My feeling overflows again. My

hope rises. You see it rising and
look away.

Your mind moderates, stops the
chain reaction. The bubbling
pond of passion cools down.
You drag me away from the
roaring sea to the safety of the
beach.

Not yet. Not yet. Says the clock.
Moments of decision come and
go and one goes on waiting for
an opportune time.

The quotidian returns with the
familiar sound of the goods train
passing by your window every night.
You ask me to catch the last train.

V

Question without Answer

What is love? You want to know.
 Your curiosity is insatiable.
 You watch *The Summer of Love.*
 Listen to Beatles. Comb through
 intimate letters and dictionaries.

You visit art galleries, see paintings,
 figures of stone, and four giant steel
 alphabets Robert Indiana erected,
 declaring that Love is red.

Love is a myth. Like truth. What is
 love is a question without an answer.
 There are as many kinds of love
 as hearts! *End of the quote.*

Love was simple in the pre-modern
age before miniskirts became a rage.
Skirts have gone, bikinis amble in
malls. Love is very different now.
Love changes every decade. Now
available in different flavours.

Love changes from place to place.
A grandfather in India, never heard
of London's swinging sixties. He tells
BBC there is no such thing as love.
"My father married me to a girl
arranged by him." We first met on
the wedding night and have stayed
together since then.

He knows not the Valentine Card.
Not seen his granddaughter looking
for boyfriends on Tinder. She respects
him but gives her own take on Love.
He says: How times have changed!

Modern or Platonic is the question.
The word Platonic fascinates you
due to its classical association. You
idealise Platonic.

But even you get second thoughts
when the Youth Elixir courses
through your veins. Enlightenment

was anti-thesis of love. The Jesuits taught
reason to undermine love. Flesh flies in
the face of Reason. In your case, that
tense state doesn't last.

You read the *Kama Sutra*. Study
digital dating that picks lovers,
matching their taste in music or
meals! Love is sourced online like
wheels and deals.

Goddess of Ambivalence, you grapple
with varieties of love, unable to decide
what to enact. Medieval, Victorian,
Edwardian, contemporary, digital,
Possessive, Angelic, or Divine Love.
Love as in Shakespeare's sonnet or
in a Plath poem. Hanif Kureishi's
all-consuming seedy suburban love
that leads to purgatory.

Stricken with dilemma, you get
stuck in the phase of transition.
The pendulum swings between
then and now and between
modern and postmodern in
literature and in life.

You dither. You fear desire as well as its
diminution. You wonder whether love is

an illusion. Inspired by the narratives of
exposure?

One woman in her time plays many parts!
You want to be a musician's muse,
a painter's plaything, a playwright's
character. Which love do you find
most attractive? Perhaps none.

Confused by varied reading, you quote
Plato that love is a search of wholeness.
Read Vatsyayan to learn that sex is
love in its beauty and glory. Do not read
its silly English translation.

You invoke Panchali. In her
name express your curiosity.,
Of the five nights, which one
did she enjoy the most? Your
words crawl all over her bare
wounded body that comes
alive fluttering in your verse.

You reimagine Sita in a poem
that you would not publish.
You have a heretic take on
Ram, the husband.

You express your yearning in
bold poems and say all that

you can't do. You shock your
readers in order to attract them!
But you evade action. Never ask
me to four-letter you. Not that
you are prudish but because
that means a great deal to you.

You cannot understand love by studying.
Experience it. You will not be a better
lover by knowing the meaning of love.
Spending years, you formulate your
Doctrine of Love, publish a book,
and be invited by American women's
clubs where fat-bosomed matrons
come to hear you.

By then, it will all be futile. I will be
of no use to you when it is cold and
I am too old. I will go away due to
decay, you will lament my passing
away. You will perhaps feel pain
and perhaps go insane.

I see life passing me by. Don't you
hear the Time's winged chariot
hurrying behind my back? As a
vernacular Marvell, I say it in
Hindi: *ko jaane kal ki, khabar nahi
hai pal ki!* So, come with me.

I stand still, paralysed by doubt.
Fear the fork in the road. This way
or that? Would you come along?

You shun the common path taken
by the text-book lovers who turn
such rooms into one-night hotels!
You believe there will be time.
Time to shut eyes, to open mouth
and suck a peach.

You are addicted to tasting life in
its fullness, richness and infinite
variety. You manipulate spare
strings and keep options open.
You will try it out with a mad man,
a seeker, a seer, an idiot, a yokel,
a pilot, a pianist, and a plumber.

You like detachment or perhaps
imagine a unique end to our story.
You want us to stage the event not
in a pokey bed-sit but in a grand
manor house with full protocol,
amid regal pomp and splendor.

Where, oh, where? A park bench,
a bomb crater, ancient falling ruins,
shining steel-glass tower, aircraft,

submarine, sailing boat, moving car
or a filthy car garage?

You are not sure. You reject all
in a row. Can't think of more.
I give up. I don't care if you want
us to lie on a hippopotamus.

I get a nightmare seeing you taste
different waters, multiple fares.
I give up. Be Tess, Emma, Anna
or Linda Loveless. Let's just get
on and come face to face.

Would you say Yes when the sun
shines, the light is right, and you lie
on grass below a green tree? Imagine
rhododendrons in your room and
a sea of roses for you to swim.

Reluctant to stage the event in
order to dodge frailty or finality?
Why do you hold back and
restrain me from raiding your
precious jewel box?

Your endless meditation on love
makes me more impatient. Still,
I tell myself all is not lost. One day,
you will conceive the unconceivable

and be tired of debating whether
desire is desirable.

I am dying to know who you are
and who I am. Where am I? And
what am I doing here? I can't make
out anything. It is all so confusing.

The city is too real for me. From
the speeding train window, I look
out for Golgonooza. Stops come
and go. There is no Golgonooza.

The train stops at Churchgate.
I walk to your Marine Drive flat,
passing by couples strolling or
sitting by the seaside.

I knock discreetly at your door.
You open it and smile. I don't bow
and scrape. I bring no flowers. You
won't have me waving a bouquet!

We are in a place as private as a grave
and yet do not embrace. You just want
to talk. And want me to be with you
only for two hours when evening turns
into night. You say as much by your
touch that is light.

So, night after night, I enter without
hope. Leaving the titillating thought
of intimacy at the door.

I am a 2021 Lover. So, I come not to
see a sumptuous, sensual scene of a
Titian painting. It is Mumbai not
Venice. I see grimy walls, crumpled
bed linen and sawdust on the floor.

Your obsession with propriety will
have a far-reaching impact on our
brand image. As a couple, when
sculptured in stone, we will not be
the Khajuraho Temple's erotic statue.

We will not look even like the sweet
couple in *Love in Montreal.* There
is no apple in my hand.

In a painting, we will be titled
Friends in a Coffee House. With no
trace of your bed in this private
room and no trace of thoughts
behind my words.

No magic lantern shows my nerves.
A lamp on the bedside stool, lighting
up *The Wasteland.* The dog-eared
paperback has lines shadowed with

penciled notes. Under Eliot lies
Virginia Woolf, in the room of her
own, saying “no need to hurry”.

You love Bloomsbury and those
who lived and loved, painted and
wrote. The prudes will say whored.
I like to read those who lived in
squares and loved in triangles.

But I cannot love a woman who
eats men like air! Virginia & Sylvia
are nice to read but I do not want
a high-strung woman who would
get inspired by their final act and
exit from life. Romance can end
at death’s door or in a grave.

Dying is a craft. Only a few can do it
themselves. Virginia fails again, and
again, before finally crossing over.

Poetry helps in time of distress but
then *The Second Coming* did lead to
a suicide attempt. Have you written
your last letter and hidden it under
the Virginia book?

I get anxious when I see a glint in
your eyes or when you walk on the

beach, smuggling stones into your
pockets to make drowning easy.

India has many unsung Sylvias who
feel with the same intensity but
cannot express themselves so well.
Those who do, never get published.

A Plath poem is not worth writing if it
costs your life. You keep reading her
and imagining the house on London's
Fitzroy Street where Yeats lived once.
See in the kitchen the gas oven in
which Sylvia Plath put her head.

Read my worry. I am nervous about
a nervous woman. I do not want her
even if she inspires me to write
The Wasteland.

Bloomsbury reinvented Love, Making
it mandatory for its residents. I do not
fantasize about Bloomsbury. Do not
experiment with modern love, paid or
free. Never try out relationships and
turn me into a Bloom.

Infidelity is fine in literature, not in life.
I draw a red line. Issue a manifesto on
our love life.

The idea is glamorous but can't have a Bloomsbury in 2021. It was founded on forbidden love. Nothing is forbidden today. I wouldn't live in Bloomsbury, with couples recruited to form triangles and hold swap parties.

In any case, they would not admit me, not grant me the permit for bed-hopping. It is granted if critics are offered a body, a body of work. I will be allowed in only if I have written books, conducted an orchestra, painted and drawn nudes that draw viewers to Tate, MOMA, and Venice.

Every eminent writer's biography makes me feel inferior. I curse my mediocrity that robs me of the moral right to seduce a friend's wife and beat my own.

I have lived a non-creative life. Betrayed no mistress. Killed no wife. Was never found drunk on the road or slumped on a dirty smelly sofa at home, buried in a sea of half-empty glasses, cigarette ends, dead roaches and yellowed newspapers.

I wear a poet's mask because you like it. Rishi Kapoor says in Hindi film *Bobby*:

Main Shayar to nahin magar aey haseena,
jabse dekha maine tujhe, mujhe shayari
aa gayi! I was not a poet till I
saw you! Became a poet on seeing you.

I was not even a lover before. Poets
and lovers are mad. I like the idea.
Want to live in Ga Ga Land but not
for long. Partake a tiny dose of insanity
that gives me a kick but does no harm.

You show in poems your body in 3-D.
I love body but like beautiful mind.
I sing a Hymn to Intellectual Beauty.

I love you more when you wear glasses.
I never got over the bespectacled face of
the Ray heroine travelling in a train in
the black-and-white fifties. Ogden Nash
was wrong.

The mind-body connection is great!
I am desperate to rummage through
your mind to reach your body, and
go where no one has gone before.

My salvation will come when you
murder and recreate yourself.

VI

You are not Understanding

I have a natural human impulse.
I indicate it in subtle ways. You
never take the hint. We go round
and round night after night. Never
reach the point of no return.

I'm at my wit's end. What to do?
Say it differently? Reveal my
intention. Be explicit. Not beat
around the bush. Come upfront?
Make a move.

Use no words or more words.
New words. Brand new words.
Gen Z words. Emotive words.

Serious words. Funny words.
Sacred words. Dirty words.

I hear word echoing in word.
I am made of words. But unlike
that poet, I cannot claim that I
can make words do what I like.
You are not understanding.

My pure Queen's English not
impressing you. OK. Now on
I using Indian English only
for moving you by conveying
my feeling. I am now Desi.
Being full Desi! As an Indian,
I shout: Down with English!
Up with the native Hinglish!

I speaking with you in our own
tongue, the language of prose
written by most Indians and
poetry written by one and only,
the super great Nissim Ezekiel.

I suspecting you are suspecting men.
Not trusting me. As a feminist you
can take it out on me. Why not
punish me for crimes committed
against your sex by my forefathers
in a very rough manner. Punishing

me is okay. Completely called for,
100 per cent. Even 200 per cent.

Pleasurefully, I imagining your
goodself riding roughshod on me,
though you a woman and I man.
I am liking idea. I am thrilling, not
angering. Enjoying your lusty busty
response. I knowing your feeling.
You are doing it not for pleasuring
but revenging. You taking me as
modern male. I taking you as
ultra-modern female. They do
it like that only in banned books.
You not reading but I reading.

You are not understanding.
I am fully standing for your full
empowerment. Not just on the
Women's Day only but on each
and every day. Recognising your
human rights. Guaranteeing all
at once and right now only.

I am not minding your having
desire, even too much of it.
I like your reading Kamala Das,
Kandasamy, even that foreign
woman Germain Greer.

Not minding your demanding
freedom to move legs or not
move them as per your desire.
Understanding properly your
improper conduct.

You can kiss below the belt,
bare your body as much as
you are liking, whenever you
are liking and wherever you
are liking.

I am always standing by with you,
just watching and saying nothing
against and not objecting.

Please bare your body for me
only and no one else, male or
female, straight or crooked,
young or old, and not when it
is cold. Your body is of gold,
good conductor of cold.
I caring for your health only.

I am giving you right now full
freedom. Welcoming you with
open arms, though I am fully
knowing that you are always
turning friends into lovers and
lovers into friends only.

You not telling me who I am.
I'm living and dying to know
that only. I am harbouring in
my heart the most uppermost
question for your frank answer.

I am always wondering why
you are never saying Yes.
Causing big disappointment.
I am questioning and then
waiting for your response
for improving our intercourse
only.

You are not hearing when like an
extremely famous foreign orator,
I am declaring: Lend me your lips
but your ears sealed to my call.

Not comparing you because you
are uncomparable. Still, thinking
of Pushpa Miss immortalized by
Nissim Ezekiel in his good poem.

Pushpa Miss departing for foreign
immediately after she attending her
lastest farewell party. Pushpa Miss
is always saying Yes. Ever ready to
do everything 'just now only'.
Nissim testified this in his poem.

But you always saying No. That is why I am tasting your external sweetness only. Never tasting your internal sweetness which must be much more tastier.

Why you always fixing fixed time for meeting me? Never preponing our meeting when I am requesting you to please kindly do it.

My feeling has no clock or fixed time. I am wanting to see you very very urgently and immediately, for much much longer than two hours only.

Two hours not sufficing. Not sufficing at all. Two hours no good. I am going without reaching the final point and completing the job.

I am paining and paining. You not imagining even one per cent. only because I am smiling. You not knowing I smiling in your front only, never in your rear.

Please read what the great Urdu poet writing about me in words

that all remembering. What is he
telling? He is telling in Urdu
on my behalf: "I am sickened but
when you coming, I am smiling,
so, you very wrongly thinking
I am healthful. No. I am smiling
only because you are coming."

Don't go by my exterior only,
touch my interior for feeling the
real me. I am differently different.
Different in my inwardly self,
different in my outwardly self.

Let me be frank. You are very very
cruel. Even Roslyn Loveless is not
loveless. You ignoring my forceful
feeling which I frequently getting

I am always applying and applying.
You never ever replying me back.
I'm tearing and tearing. You never
wiping tears on my face with your
tongue. Not hearing me, not seeing
me. You are blind or what.

You talking like a poet but counting
like a bank clerk, calculating profit
and loss of going all the way and
deciding in favour of not. I telling

you what a poet should count by
quoting Elizabeth: "How do I love
Thee? Let me count the ways."

My another question to you. If
wild in your poems then why not
with me. A poet's persona much
differing from her real persona.
You are one in arts and the other
in life! I awaiting your wildness.
Be wild at least tomorrow night
if not wanting to do tonight.

I am nightly reading your wild
poem in my bed. The poem is
moving me. Shaking each and
every part of my whole body.
Waking up my nervous system
with pull and push, pull and
push, pull and push. You are
not understanding what I am
hinting and hinting.

You poeting when chores sparing.
Writing love poetry but not loving.
Meditating on love and emotions,
dissecting feeling, commenting on
climax without climaxing. You are
knowing love but not making it.

Only reading and reading, doing
nothing with me or even with
yourself in solitude.

You so unmerciful and sans heart.
If it is there, not working. It is
disabled by your overactive head.
You bothering about your head
only. I am fully knowing because
you telling me I am eating your
head. I shall eat it up so that you
focus on you heart only.

Head is the enemy of heart, the
seat of Love. You think Love is
living in the head. Shakespeare
himself was unsure where fancy
is bred, in the heart or in the head.

Would my brain flutter if you kiss?
No. You wanting me to say I love
you from the bottom of my brain?
You will say that unification of
sensibility is not possible. In that
case, choose feeling not intellect.
You will then feel what I feel.

My inner voice comes from my heart.
My seeing you is not for timepass but
a must for my living. If denied, I am

harakiring my entire self from top to bottom, right now and right here in front of your eyes, at your fair feet.

I am watching your reaction. You are not crying after hearing such moving words coming out of my pathetic mouth. Shockingly, you laughing and laughing. Laughing at my instant poetry or what?

Myself liking laughter which is my medicine as you have consigned me to this eternal waiting room.

But your laughing is insulting to late but great poet Nissim Ezekiel. I was meeting Nissim in Bombay, not Mumbai. As an aspiring writer of rising renown, I showing him a book review written by me on my own. He appreciating it. Especially liking my using the word "screw".

I wondering why he liking such dirty words. I silent before that literary hero. Nissim Ezekiel not amidst us today but still inspiring to budding poets.

I am carrying his flag for which
I am bound to be recognized one
day in the annals of Indian poetry.
My *Rhapsody in Hinglish* will be
prescribed by universities world
over in courses under the head:
Exotic Literature! It will be hit
like exotic food sold in expensive
restaurants and specialty shops.

My being an Indian poet was a minus
point earlier but now a big plus point.
I will be starred by a famous dramatist
to strut on the vast global stage as the
Lover-in-waiting! All will be liking me
as another Prince Charles.

I digressing for drowning my sorrow.
Conjuring up a rosy future only for
distracting me from the crisis caused
by your not saying Yes.

This internal crisis is caused by your
hesitant self. But there is an external
crisis caused by the political rascal
and his Disease Control Authority
started for eradicating lovesickness
from the whole of Hindu society.
His police roundups couples and

suppresses what is now called Love Jihad. Hating is a holy mission. Loving a deadly sin!

His vigilantes violating modesty of the innocent maidens going into bar toilets to get themselves deflowered. These thugs barge into beer bars, drag modest maidens out and thrash them in public. People do nothing, just watch the spectacle and cheer.

Vigilantes hanging in the Hanging Gardens and harassing coupling couples. Exposing their names in social media for the benefit of their fathers. Even shooting couples with mobiles and viralising their dirty compromising photos and videos.

Rascals bothering with our private business and coming in our *beech*, middle. None of their business when you willing and I more than willing.

We are doing nothing inside your private room except chatting and chatting. Our intercourse is pure, proper and innocent also. They are knowing this through their sources

always watching us when we sitting
or strolling by seaside, not holding
hands or kissing unlike others.

Not that you are caring about Them.
You are bold. Not worrying about
Mobs, carrying on intercourse only
with me without fear at night. Let
them do their worst. We are not
running away from this sacred land
of the Khajuraho Temple's erotic
statu*es* and the *Kama Sutra*.

If the rascals confront us, I will
impress them by loudly shouting
Jai Sri Ram again and again and
denouncing St. Valentine as a
western seller of cards. They will
understand my slogans against the
foreign saint as they have been
taught his name for the political
agitation against the Valentine Day.

I will utter a few words in Sanskrit
about our better Love God Sri Sri
Kam Deva. They will then see you
as a *sanskari* girl with a devotee
and go after the next couple.

What to do. This is the only way
to survive in a weird place where
an armed Anti-Love Jihad Force
has been given powers to arrest
without warrant.

Worry not about the situation
affecting us and other couples
doing very bad things in front
of the good people of Mumbai.

Change is coming! When Liberal
Government coming, all rascals
running with tails between their
legs and disappearing completely.

A big change sweeping even you.
Your hesitation going away like
anything. Outer climate changing.

Your internal climate changing.
Frozen Himalayas melting. You
melting into my arms, dripping
all over myself and yourself.

You becoming wilder by the night.
Telling me that the night is young.
Asking me to stay, not go. Saying
don't go! Stopping me by catching

my arm. Barring my way by digging
your swollen breasts into my chest.

Promising and even offering me
luscious fruits of your secret garden.
With this very same Yours Truly,
you gladly going all the way and
surrendering to me your precious
possession that you protecting for
very long. One day! One day!

Why smiling? Am I dreaming or
what? This time, my dream is
very topical and realistic also.

Wait and see. A giant tsunami
coming, affecting not just us but
whole Mumbai to be ruled by the
Free Love Party. The voters are
fed up with the Free Hate Party.

BEST company issuing a circular
asking passengers to indulge in
lip kissing in their red buses, like
they do in the London buses. Red
is the colour of Love. So, all do.

Mumbai is turned into London.
In coming free-for-all, everyone
merrily kissing. No one ever

stopping or staring. Mumbai is modern, even ultra-modern.

This revolution arriving in very near future. Coming not because of men but because women at long last not taking it lying down but standing up and giving it. They are all rebelling, tearing off the veil and demonstrating very openly and demanding what they really want.

Women are marching on the streets with flags, shouting smutty slogans, protesting in public, promoting their private thoughts and parts. The famous monologue is heard loud and clear by all as a stirring clarion call!

VII

You are You, and I ...

To understand the real you,
 I look for a model to model
 you on. Not possible to find
 one and arrive at an answer.
 Can't catch the enigmatic you.

I continue to try day and night
 to study this elusive woman.
 Is she a modern rebel-girl in a
 Bombay flat, sitting under Che's
 visage, singing a protest song,
 pointing her accusing finger?

Holding a glass, between puffs,
 she looks me in the eye, winks,

beckons, grabs, drags, stops at
nothing! Shatters taboos, breaks
boundaries. Is that she?

Do I see a traditional *sanskari*
girl who knows when to stop?
She terminates my crucial move
with a jerk. Never crosses the line
drawn in her mind like in stone.
Makes me leave every night.
Who is she? Can't pigeonhole
her since she navigates with
ease between two worlds.

Still, I want to brand her, not
with a hot tool. I brand her as
a postmodern radical writer.
No good for me. As writer she
is very outgoing. As woman,
she stops herself halfway.

She is no 18th century heroine
in a flowing gown, a beauty
obsessed with her beau. She is
no bimbo in a bikini, prancing
around, doing nothing.

La Belle Dame Sans Merci!
I see the message she flashes.

"Talk to me, don't do. Look
at me, don't touch."

The power of the forbidden!
It flares me up. She wants to
see whether her restraint fuels
my sensual hunger?

Who is she? She should know
that even the Victorian edicts
were ignored. They all went
ahead, merrily doing everything
they wanted. The legs of tables
were kept covered at night but
women's legs were bared.

Alas, for her a glance is all but
it heightens my tension and
frustration. My world does not
change by a glance.

She sees desire as the goal,
and fear that the actual will
disenthrall your soul! *With
apologies to a woman poet.*

You like my words and let me
touch you with words. But my
words do not go far. Lead us
nowhere. These fall inadequate.

So, I borrow: "You see years
of crowded passion in a word
and half a life in a sentence!"
I don't wish to end with words.
I await a wordless fevered night.
The tyranny of words must end.
We are not lost for words but
getting lost because of words.

We now say words that do not
have our own voices. I want to
go back to the age when voice in
us communicated without saying
a word. *Borrowed from Latin.*

The only words that I want to hear
from you are two: 'Don't Go.'
These are said by a Bengali heroine
during a tryst in her room at night.

A Hindi heroine, who asks the hero
to stay sings: *abhi to raat jawan hai.*
'The night is still young'. You never
say that. I am forced to leave your
warm room every night. I feel being
driven out in the cold.

You talk of transcendental love
and transactional love. Don't
know the first. Is the latter love

made between the soiled sheets
of an accountant's bed?

You dislike lust, separate it from
love, show your interest in true
love, whatever that is. I make no
such distinction. I solicit you.
You solicit my comments as if
that is why we meet. We need
no pretense. We don't have to
declare that we meet at night to
discuss the world's plight.

Let them talk. They will talk.
It is their business to talk.
Jagjit Singh sings: *Kuch to log*
kahenge, logo ka kam hai kehna.
Abandon caution.

The banquet of ideas brings us
closer but scotches your craving,
suppresses emotions and keeps
us apart. Ideas move the world,
not the heart that has its reason
that reason cannot fathom.

My heart cannot bear the burden
of ideas. Mindfulness prevents the
cracking of cautious composure.
Sensation is lost in thought.

Girls find hard to cope with this.
They write poetry and suppress
the conflict. You try to resist
hesitation, but never give in to
temptation.

Indian woman is dead and new
Indian Woman struggling to be
born. You are still caught in the
belief that the heart must always
be governed by mind so that it
knows when it misses a beat and
how to stop an irregular beat.

The curse of the intellect! A battle
rages within you. Not your fault.
You are gifted with a western body
and an Indian mind! Between the
East and West, you are lost because
of your bi-cultural upbringing that
caused confusion.

You took to the school tiffin of messy
sambhar-bhat and ate with girls who
had sandwiches. You played lyre and
learnt Jane Eyre. In the annual festival,
you acted in *Lady Windermere's Fan.*

At home, you were told to recite
the Gita and imitate Sita and Savitri.

Every night discreetly, you read
Mills and Boon but because of the
sisters, never dreamt of the tall, dark
and handsome man.

Later, you went to the co-ed college
that had no holy sisters. There you
were waylaid by Anna Karenina and
Molly Bloom. They taught you what
you had not known before. You saw
love superseding dignity as giggling
girls shared naughty tales.

The holy sisters taught you to read.
Here Anna & Molly told you to feel.
Feel his lips feeling you all over. They
unwrapped man for you. Inserted him
into your dreams. Anna & Molly
taught you desire, deception and the
four-letter word.

You studied literature. You know
that we exist because we feel. Had
you done commerce in college, you
won't be seeing a fellow like me.

Produced and shaped by the text,
we must love and be lost.
You are fragmented, you need the
one who turns you into whole.

You do not like Bollywood films.
Deride these as vulgar and kitsch.
Call Umrao Jan a courtesan.

If you want, I am ready to mimic
the hero of a European art film
and give you a passionate kiss.
Kisses in art films go on and on.
Let us do those.

Lovers in art films gladly court
separation. Do you Like that?
Will you do what they do. Will
you exit with a smile? Or look
back in anger?

You say art films are refined,
without a set formulaic end.
Knife in the Water stiffens your
back in the Anandam Hall.
In other theatres, couples sing
and dance, then exit without
kissing, to live happily ever after.

The masses have only Bollywood
for ready reference, frenetic daily
consumption and emulation.
Like life, Bollywood bristles with
contradictions. It serves lust with
spirituality. *The Dirty Picture* has

the song *Mera Ishq Sufiana!*
Hindi films reflect social mores.
The ever-pining, hapless, helpless,
heroine begs for hero's heart. She
pants in her tight red choli, her
breasts heave due to breathless
dancing, not by hero's touching.

She falls on his feet, begging for
his kind attention. Anna Karenina
tells her that respect was invented
to cover the empty place where
love should be.

Wind blows, lightning strikes, it pours
cats and dogs because the filmgoers
want to see the heroine drenched, with
the wet blouse showing curves more
clearly. She gets marooned with the
handsome hero on a deserted island.

The heroine breaks into her sixth
song, remaining prim and proper,
with the hero wanting to touch her
elusive fair flesh. The rest is left to
the wild imagination of the viewers.

They know the Government rules
do not allow the hero to go far.
They are contended to watch the

human union depicted by flowers
and butterflies buffeted by breeze.

They go home humming the item
girl's song. They will come to watch
the film again tomorrow to enhance
their understanding of love and lust.

Is true love like what is depicted in a
Bollywood film? You ask me. Why
blame Bollywood alone? Do you see
life in the royal balcony when Queen
Elizabeth appears in full regalia with
the mandated made-up face, and her
husband. Can one suspect a congress
between them that procreates?

You protest against hypocrisy and
oppression of women. Your blood
boils against injustice. You hitch up
your petticoat and tear up your sari
to wave a flag of revolt! Suspense
mounts, TV cameras roll, wanting
to see more of your reddened flesh.

Your slogans shatter silence and
secrecy. You bring to life passive
objects walking as Indian women
and inspire them to march.

You are no Bollywood woman.
Not even Indian. You don't sing
of things you want done unto you.
You declare what you will do!
All in theory because in practice
you do nothing. But your threat
frightens the poor Indian male.
I am different as you will find
when I take you differently.

Come, take your lustful revenge!
I would love it. Then at last,
I shall be able to do it to you.
Come after me with bare fangs.
Dig deep into my flesh. Suck
my blood. Let its river flow.

I am waiting. Come, come and
take it out on me. Give me, give
me, your anger. Give me hate.
Give me love. All that you have.
Give me all of you.

VIII

My name is...

How can you understand me?
You did not ask for my biodata
before letting me into your room.
Tonight, I introduce myself and
tell you how I grew up, though
may say the process is not over.

I was admitted to school to get
me deracinated. Recited nursery
rhymes, kissed a girl at the age
of four and got applauded for it.

In the college, my economics
lecturer, obsessed with the Gross
National Product, was a beauty.

We feasted on her bare midriff.
She wore no top, only sari. You
are never topless though I in my
sleep see you as you should be.

The poetry professor quoted poems
without feeling. He did not move
us. Still, we loved English poetry.

The affair was not one-sided.
English poets loved India. Eliot,
Shelley saw India from afar.
Kathleen Raine wrote about it.
Marvell envisioned his coy
mistress by the Ganges. Eliot
brought the Ganges into his
poem. Eliot studied our sacred
texts. Walt Whitman wrote
A Passage to India!

The English Romantics taught
me romancing. The modernists
exposed me to modernism and
the ills of our new world.

Without English poets, I wouldn't
have known how to see you and
what to say to you. They taught
me ways of seeing and saying.

A sounding cataract of England,
not of the Himalayas, haunts me.
Four Seasons mean foreign music.
The colours I see are not seen in
India. I dream of you dancing in
a field of daffodils. I envision a
tall English rock just to see you
standing against it.

I borrowed words and said:
"*Let us go...*" and we went on
our first ride, you clutching me.
I said *the Last Ride Together.*
You enjoyed the poem. In that
beginning was my end.

English literature shaped me.
I feel English at times. But I am
Indian. A morning coat does not
choke my desire, nor does the
afternoon tea drown it! No
yellow fog envelopes my house.
The bright sun shines over me.

Don't kiss me if you don't want.
Look at me. A verse runs across
my forehead. It snatch wanders
through my brain.

I am no poet but I want to attract
you with a poem or two. Address
you as fair but frozen maid. My
poems are not perfect. Like that
Austen heroine, you must offer
to 'repair my pen'. I will let you
do it unlike the hero who replies:
"I can do it myself."

A poem is entwined with my heart.
Like the yellow creeper suffocating
the tree from which it cannot be
pulled apart. You are that poem!
I see you in a red-bordered sari,
under a Red Oleander on the bank
of the Padda, caressing wet black
hair. I approach you silently on a
white sailing boat under a blue sky!
You are singing a song suffused
with sorrow.

You ask me in Bengali: *What do you
want from me?* Do you really say that
or I put it in your mouth? I reply: *I do
not want. I want nothing.* Mystified,
you ask: *Why do you then call me to
this wilderness?* Are you a poet, you
ask me. Only a poet wants nothing;

others want me and my everything,
you say. A poet dies declaring his love.

I fall back on a poem. Call you *Devi*!
Devi who is *Nari* or *Nari* who is *Devi*!
What do you want? You ask me again.
Do you seek *Devi*'s boon or *Nari*'s face
like moon? Are you a devotee or man?

You prompt me to make a move that
I do not make. You guess my move.
Tick me off in English: *Don't be silly.*

Strange that while with you, I hear a
language that is not yours, nor mine!
Intimate feeling is best expressed in a
foreign tongue, also used to convey
rejection with ease.

I try to impress you with borrowed
words, verse, ideas, and voices.

Connect with you through a third
party, a living medium and a dead
modem. Nothing works.

Who should I be? A drunken poet?
Borrow a role from some famous
play. I cannot do English Theatre.

I play Indian roles. I am Devdas,
the hard-drinking hero. No. I'm
Ashok Kumar, the long-haired
monk in saffron robes. I turn my
back on you and walk away. Be
my Meena Kumari for that role!

From the reel world, I descend into
the real world of your room. I am
Sahir, you are Amrita. I am Farooq,
you are Shabana.

Alas, no white smoke floats in this
dream sequence. I end my reverie.

I do not want to be in a far-away
world where you reach me only
by sending a smoke signal from
my cigarette butt. And from where
I cannot touch you.

I pick Sahir-Amrita because Indian
students have done in the English
Bard and his young Italian couple.
I do not want to look up to you in
a balcony beyond my reach.
I am put off by that couple by an
erudite critic who comments:
"The libidinal impulses of Romeo
and Juliet being reciprocal, they

activated their individual erotic
drivers and integrated them..."

Nor do I identify with Heer Ranjha,
the famous folk lovers of Punjab.

Me and my multiple roles! I am
a Baul singer, the mystic minstrel
who roams around the countryside
playing a one-string instrument.
I sing, someone hears me or hears
me not. *Borrowed from Tagore.*
No. I can't be a singer. My voice
will make them laugh.

Be an exilic writer commanding
luminous prose plus a slave-woman.
Exile is not possible for me.
Oh, God! Who should I be? I'm
having more difficulty than the
student who tells the father that
he would be a doctor.

Nothing is possible for a man such
as me. A man without talent. Man
with no money, no power and no
network. Mr. Nobody. A man of
absolutely no consequence.

This world has no place for me. The world is what it is! What to do? Spend days sitting in my flat, in a pensive pose, drinking all by myself. Nurse desire while the half-burnt cigarette sets fire to the blue tablecloth embroidered with burnt holes. I keep watching the holy smoke rise.

I spend nights in the Park Street Club wearing a white jacket and black trousers, unrolled. I am too drunk to dance properly. I am an actor who performs while drunk.

I must be seen performing, singing, screaming, staggering, stammering, sleepwalking, abusing, cursing, beating the bearer, breaking bottles, waving a half-empty glass, tearing a silk curtain, grabbing a belly-dancer, hugging a half-clad woman and a half-mad man, kissing the chosen few, hitting a pillar, shattering the shiny mirror and creating a mega scene for being watched by millions. Cheered by my current and former lovers, I go on singing: *This is life*! *This is Life!* Like the hero in that Bengali film.

I be Lazarus and you Jesus. Upon
your touch, blood starts flowing
again in my dead veins.

I am a Hindu priest with long
hair, sitting cross-legged in a
sacred pose performing *havan*,
stoking the all-consuming leaping
flames, pouring *ghee* and reciting
in God's tongue *Bhasmantagvam*
Shariram.

All shall be ashes one day. I pray,
empower me to eat a peach before
that happens to me and you! The
grave's a fine and private place,
but none, I think, do there embrace.

Reciting the Sanskrit mantra,
I feel like the real me, speaking
from my heart, seeing a cloud in
every silver lining, seeing us
dance in fire!

Tonight you speak to me but
again you are not really with me.
Will it be a different night
tomorrow? I keep hoping but
tomorrow never comes.

IX

In Their Eyes

I said a lot about myself. I may claim to be this, that or the other but only they have the power to define me. How they see me matters. We are not what we may think we are. We are what they see us as.

My creator knows me but less than the critics. If Eliot were to read his critics today, he would learn a lot about his J. Alfred Prufrock.

Eliot saw his world shattered and grieved about it. Today, if I read newspapers I see India lying etherized upon the table while surgeons are sedated and asleep.

Anesthesia invented in 1846. Prufrock published in 1915. A century has gone since then. New times call for revisions and re-revisions. Await a 21st century Eliot, tuned to post-modern sensibility, will in his new Love Song make a distinction between the time past and time present and respond to the crisis of today.

New Eliot has to have a new name for his new lover. Old names have gone unfashionable. No one by the name of Prufrock is found today.

The New Lover does not hesitate. Reveals his intention at the outset. Feels adequate, sure of himself. Does not fear rejection. He is at ease with reality and women.

He is not afraid of approaching old age. He knows the world itself will end soon. He wants instant pleasure and wants to get it over with during the very first night.

Today Eliot comes and witnesses
a million battles instead of the War.
Sees unending low-level violence
instead of a mega massacre. He
observes ills of this century and
responds. Eliot gets transformed
by contemporary times and writes
an equally powerful poem.

Death has undone so many, Dante
and Eliot exclaimed. Since then, life
has surpassed death. Life undoes
many more. The dead dead fall in
numbers, the living dead keep rising.

The critics are conditioned to see
me in the light of what Eliot wrote
a century ago. I can quote their
chapters on my verse. They model
me on Prufrock. I look like him
and am in a similar love situation.

They have a point. A century lies
between us but I and Prufrock have
the same human impulses and same
personal worries about the balding
head and spindly legs.

The Prufrock Temperament marks me
out. It affects my relationship with you

which goes nowhere and leaves me
frustrated. Prufrock doubts if he would
ever succeed with his woman. So, do I.

Critics turn to Prufrock in order to
investigate me. See me as a masterpiece
of representation, somewhat anonymous,
unexceptional, unheroic, and physically
unremarkable.

My questions are unanswerable, says
one critic. No wonder you do not
answer any. He says my facelessness
is my presence. To him, I am eternally
recognisable. Everything to everyone.
"This redeems him for us." Another
critic takes a very different view.
He says my profundity sets me apart.

Critics study my monologue. They see
me seeking you every night and you not
letting me enter you. It demolishes my
standing as man. I am called a coward.

They say I am hesitant and unsure as
I am Indian. They forget that the most
famous English lover did not dare?
He did not dare to eat a peach or walk
naked upon the beach. Could not force

the moment to its crisis. In short, he
was afraid.

"I'm no Prince Hamlet..." He said that
to diminish his importance. But he was
like the Prince of Denmark and so am I.
Like Hamlet, we know that action differs
from acting. Do I not act in your room?

Like Prufrock, I too do not think highly
of myself. I'm brown. He was white, but
his blood was red. So is mine. Our Love
is same to same. I too get no response.

Can't blame you. Perhaps it is my fault.
Dogged by dissolution, like Prufrock,
I lament my lack of qualities. That
lover knew he was not being heard.

I too cannot convey my feelings to you.
They see me trying night after night
and failing. I am alone. No one sings
to me. No one will sing to me.

Prufrock is worse than me. He
presumes he would fail. Imagines
her indifference. Never dares to
express his love. Never tries to find
her response. Makes no effort at all.

I perceiver. Show courage to chase
you with words alluding to my love.
Suffer your hesitation every night.
So, my self-doubt is justified.

Prufrock faces silence which she never
breaks. He has no words from her to
weave into his song. He mouths his
creator's concerns by referring to the
Yellow Fog and a patient etherized
upon the table. You speak to me. I
cite your words though they are not
about me. At least, we communicate.

Prufrock's song came in the midst of
a social upheaval caused by the war.
I sing in the time of a political crisis.
My song is influenced by your politics.

I like the insertion of topicality into
a Love Song. It is needed in this
day and age. Afterall, I am not a lover
of the romantic era. I'm post-modern
and like you, believe politics is
personal. I know that critics will
comment on this aspect of my Song.

If my tale ends differently, critics will
attribute that not to my character but
to the plot, to some event that did not

take place in Prufrock's life. They say
I and Prufrock have the same flaw.

They find it ironic that a man with a
name such as J. Alfred Prufrock sings
a Love Song. My name is Anand, I
can sing and yet cannot snatch a kiss.

My monologue is fed into computers
that pick the most-used words to detect
my mental state during our nocturnal
meetings. Keywords, linked to feeling
and meaning, are discussed in classes.

Armed with this data, critics unpeel
my psychic layers and scrutinise my
character. I am taken apart. They say
I prevaricate, never come to the point.
They highlight my dilemma, find me
awkward, timid, insecure, intimidated,
plaintive and indecisive. They see me
distraught as you suppress your desire.

I am called Gen X Prufrock. Another
critic says it is an insult to Gen X.
Kak never takes an initiative. Even the
19th century heroes were always quick
to join at the hips.

If Kak was unable to say it, he could have sexted her. WhatsApped an explicit selfie, baring himself and his feeling for her. Could have messaged or massaged her. Kak did nothing. He just enjoyed vain intellectual chatter and went home every night.

Another critic is empathetic. He points out that Kak was unlucky to have fallen for an Indian woman of a rare kind! Not many such left in 2021.

The New Indian woman would have come to the point in the first few minutes, pre-empted Kak, aborted his Love Song and silenced him with a never-ending kiss.

Some say Kak is not very different from Prufrock. Kak has the mindset of Prufrock. Had he not been so, he would cry for lust, not sing a song. He never promises her a rose garden. Some critics say I am Prufrock of the post-truth age. Is it a compliment?

They ridicule Prufrock for being shy of women and wanting to be embraced by mermaids. Similarly, Prufrock,

does not dare to see women without
borrowed glasses, they say.

They are right. I feel scared of women
and their sophisticated chatter. I feel
more inadequate in their company.

I live in fear of hearing you say: That
is not what I meant. That is not what
I meant at all. My awkwardness and
anxiety are caused by lack of fulfilment.

Am I neurotic like Prufrock? I accuse!
I accuse! You made me neurotic, gave
me the Prufrock Complex. Afflicted
me with maladies. Made me waste a
lifetime, coping with your hesitation.

I ought to have ignored your hesitation.
But had I forced our play's denouement
and myself on you, a feminist would
have killed me with her poison pen.

Politics distracted you from me but it
enriched my song as I picked powerful
words from your statements. I inserted
India into the song, making it topical.

An American critic, who lived in India,
and loves Bollywood, says Kak quotes

film songs with reverence that Prufrock shows towards Latin sayings and Biblical stories. Such a poem had to come out of the collective Indian mind enthralled by Bollywood songs.

He tells the West-centric scholars that Kak didn't need T. S. Eliot guiding him to write a love song. Kak inherited the ancient tradition of Sanskrit love poetry.

A teacher teaching English as foreign language lauds my Indian English for its diversity and cultural vibrancy. She says had Prufrock spoken it, he would have re-energised poetry, made it less stagnant and English poets less fatigued. She causes a huge furor. American poets protest. They claim their poetry is robust and they are far from fatigued! The controversy boosts the market for Am-Indians teaching creative writing.

A critic borrows Ezra Pound's words to say that Kak's verses are poetry that is news that stays news. He says Kak assimilates knowledge into his poem, weaving beautifully the contemporary with the perennial!

An Indophile calls me Eliot reborn in India! His rival shoots back: An Indian Eliot! An oxymoron! Eliot has to be born in America and made in England. Eliot cannot be transposed to India.

A critic says Eliot liked revisions, so he reappeared as Kak and wrote a new version of his song! The rebirth theory catches on. Eliot wanted to be Indian. Studied Vedanta. Ended a poem with *Shantih shantih shantih.*

Kak is feted in Silicon Valley as an innovator, who tapped the creative potential of Lockdown Love Life! A foreign journal prints the face of a woman and says *She Dithered and Dithered.*

Why am I called Indian Prufrock? Prufrock should be called British Kak.

Foreign critics are nice, Indian critics are nasty. English poets promote Indian talent. Indian poets are too busy to nurture young poets. No Ezra Pound is found in India.

Despite what I did to help critics, some
say my song is not poetry! I say to them
drink deep or taste not the Pierian spring.
I use Sanskrit words in my Song to make
their papers appear scholarly.

Have I digressed? You put me off
saying: That's not what I meant.
That is not what I meant at all.

I repeat these here to fox my critics.
Let them divine the meaning of what
you said or meant. You too will be
thoroughly analysed. They will regret
that they have no word from you
that can be used as testimony.

They will brand me as a conflicted
soul and go on to misread me in
different ways. I tell critics that I
dared to come to you. If I were as
dejected or fearful as Prufrock,
would I have joined you every
night even after seeing no chance
of consummation?

Let critics debate the ifs and buts of
our personal history and draw their
own conclusions. Let them puzzle

over my song, beat it with a hose to
find what it means.

Who I am is a mystery that they
cannot solve. Pass your judgement
on me as lover-man.

I stand on Prufrock's shoulders. He
made critics take note of me. It is
because of Prufrock that an eminent
publisher would publish my song
instead of flinging it at me, calling it
'insanity'.

Prufrock talks of drowning but in
reality lives on. A metaphorical
death! Prufrock never dies! Like
God, he is everywhere. He has an
unerring presence in reviews, essays,
poetry, fiction, and crime fiction.

I am no Prufrock. My days are
numbered. I fear death. I fear
after-life.

X

Night of the Scorpion!

It happens when least expected.
One night turns out to be the
Qatal ki Raat. Or shall I call it
the night of the long knife?

I enter your room, having no idea
how different the night will turn
out to be and what it will do to us.

Your light bulb attracts me like *shama*
draws the moth. This theme features
in Urdu poetry. *Shama* always burns
its lover. This moth survives nightly
exposure to the candle flame.

Nothing should have been different.
You have a set routine of heady talk,
no action. I accept that as inevitable.

Tonight, your fair, bare braceleted
arm moves. No, not to pull my face
nearer. It reaches out to switch the
radio on.

A third voice enters the room!
Conversation was flagging.
To keep it going, that voice was
needed. My excitement dies.
I dislike the third. When we walk,
I see a shadow walking with us.

The radio comes on. The music
stops abruptly. It announces a
loud dire warning. A screaming
ambulance is heard. Racing with
a body, neither alive nor dead.

The radio announcer, like a firing
gun, lets out three dreadful words:
Disease Death Lockdown.

Lockdown? What lockdown?
We wonder. We shudder. Our
eyes get locked. It dawns on us.
We are Locked in! Locked in.

I cannot leave you tonight.
I shall be with you.
With you, the whole night.
The whole night! Together.
Alone.

Outside, the sky goes black.
The street deserted. Human
forms vanish. Voices silenced.
All movement banned. City
drops dead. Certainty gone.
We remain.

In the room, with one bed and one
pillow, we are twinned, rendered
secure. Doing nothing. Watching
each other in fear and hope.

Stuck with each other for the whole
night, pinned to the bed, wriggling!
Tied together! Safe from the world!

Exciting to be caught without my
pajamas and toothbrush. A couple
sang in the film *Bobby*: *Hum tum
ek kamre mein band hon, aur chabi
kho jaye!* We two get locked in a
room and the key gets lost!

The world stopped! Life on hold.
You like the idea. Felt life was too
much with you.

The radio lists the number of deaths.
The grim voice pierces like the
menacing sound of approaching
bombers in a war.

Your room turns into a safe air-raid
shelter. The impending disaster
quickens your pulse, sparks ecstasy.
The voice stings you. Turns you on.

Anticipation descends through our
spines, reaches other parts. We feel
a frisson of fear. Fear kept us apart.
Fear brings us together.

Phobos and Eros jump into our playpen!
We mortals feel honoured to be guided
by visitors from the famed Classical
World! They say we are with you two.
Their mother hovers over, eggs us on.
Do what you did not do for so long!

Phobos and Eros work their magic.
My body blood-shot, veins swollen.
Our lips twitch. Every cell radiates
desire and dread. I feel red.

Red of heat. I see red, red of cheeks,
red of rose, red of love, red of the
blood rushing in feverish veins.

We can look no longer. We blink,
come closer. Your heat seeks me,
turns me into a shooting missile.
I get overwhelmed. Bubbling.

Excuse me, in this state, cannot
continue in an even tone. If I do
not stop, I will start blabbering
like a drunk. I change the topic.
Interrupt the narrative. I'm too
excited to narrate the event.
I have to wait. I shall resume
when passion is spent and calm
of mind returns.

Let me first deal with the troubling
questions sparked by the historic
event that hit the two of us in a
dark room.

When I resume the story after a
brief interruption, I will tell all.
Hide nothing. Will tell all.

XI

Narrativus Interruptus

The troubling questions.
How long will the fever last?
Is it the beginning of the end?
Or the end of the beginning?
And how will it end?

How do I describe the climax?
The title for my Love Song?
Night Thoughts. No. Can't
steal the title. The BBC would
sue me. I must look for another.

The heat of the moment has
overcharged not only my heart
but also my mind.

I continue wordplay. Wait for
you to drag me away. At last,
you sound like the desperate
Eliza Doolittle who screamed
'Words. Words. Words'. This
is an entirely new you.

We are partners in crime. You love
words. I too like playing with words.
The load of words about you that I
carry incapacitates me. I try to go
beyond words but you never help.

A miracle happens. We get carried
to the After-Words stage. You lose
control of yourself. Get transported
to a wordless world.

Like Mary you seemed to say:
"Now I go into silence." Words
hamper action, silence leads to
action. We both get tongue-tied
for the first time.

Products of the text, we end its
tyranny, discard wordy wisdom,
become aware that words break
under tension, slip, slide and
perish. Decay with imprecision.
I borrow words for effect.

We discover a world beyond
words. Learn to do without
words. We move beyond
language and begin a direct
dialogue, a dialogue without
words. We lapse into silence.

True lovers speak the language
of eyes. They can communicate
through eyes. While scientists
investigate brain-to-brain
interface, poets sing about
eyes-to-eyes interface.

We share thoughts unmediated
by language. Thoughts, unlike
words, are hard to manipulate.
Our exchanges become pure.

Our struggle with words ends.
No more do I need words for
you. But I have to use words
for those wanting and waiting
to know what happened to us.

Now a question crops up in
my mind. If I were lost in you
and captivated by all-consuming
love, then how come I am able
to narrate all this?

Unlike Sanjay, I am a fighter in
the battle. Yet, I transmit live,
using apt words and images.
Am I one or two? One fighting,
the other observing and
narrating.

One never stops watching. The
mind is not shut off when tongue
and mouth work and we are
otherwise engaged! Why does
one remain watchful at moments
when nothing else should matter.

Does it not amount to adultery.
Is nothing complete? Is nothing
sacred?

I should skip such vain comments
and describe the bed-shaking act.
Ultimately, an event changed your
mind. Your long-preserved virginity
and my lust did not turn to dust.
You did not let love down.

Your caution inside the room did
not protect our privacy. We got
known as lovers. Your landlord
the liftman and neighbours know.

Your Platonic partnership only
ensured that we were not called
Live-in Partners.

They would see change in our eyes.
Such events do not remain secret.
How will they see us now? Let's
us imagine. We are celebrated in
folklore, sung by poets, admired
by sons rebelling against fathers
and daughters wanting freedom.

We feature in classrooms. Scholars
probe us, explain why we acted so
behind closed doors. Students
wonder why we fail to hook up in
a closed room night after night.
We are maligned by the prudish.

Kamini Kaushal in a film with
Dileep Kumar stops her tears lest
her love story gets exposed and they
get maligned. She sings: *Badnaam*
na hojaaye mohabbat ka fasana!

Reviewers are cruel. They want to
know how old I was when I met you.
Critics comment on my age. They
investigate what my family was like?

In which town did I grow up? They
read our letters. Burn the letters.

They collect adulterated crumbs
in the archives and reach flawed
conclusions. Critics go by myths.
Dons misinterpret. They write
rubbish and we are not there to
say: That is not what we meant.
We were not that at all!

One silly critic says my lover
being Indian, I had a harder nut
to crack. You are identified as
Indian because you take time
to touch. You are a dignified
teacher of sterling character
because you hesitate. No one
blames you.

Reviewers are confused and want
to write clever things. In our case,
they are handicapped because
Prufrock presents no model to
compare you with. He hides
his woman. She never speaks to
Prufrock. I show you. You speak
to me and I record and reveal
your words.

We live on in journals run by
psychoanalysts. I like gravitas.
Would love to figure in seminars
in Cambridge, Oxford, and Yale.

Don't you see it as an end better
than being sung about in Punjab
villages or shown on Instagram
as a smutty couple?

I monetise our affair without your
having to kiss and tell. My words
provide a feast for the heart, mind,
eyes and ears when approached
through an audio book.

I present my monologue at the
Jaipur Literature Festival where
they go in droves to see writers
perform. JLF forces even dour
writers on to the stage.

Their performance poetry sessions
are popular. My song with light
and sound effects will be sold-out.
I shall include every bit about us.
A haiku of 17 syllables is of no
use to JLF.

Charming JLF women come and go,
exclaiming: Kak is lovely! Isn't he?
His song is so sweet, his smile so
lovely. I must have him for dinner,
says a coiffed head. She might have
me for breakfast too. She is Larkin's
bitch who reads nothing but *Which*!

Daunted by her scent and sight,
I dare not meet her at night.
I do not know how to greet her.
Shake her by which hand, kiss her
on the lips or cheeks. Which cheek
first? An existential question.
I dread sophisticated women and
their vain fashionable chatter.

You are you. Your words and your
gestures are genuine. You do not
come and go talking for effect.
And at last, you showed me the
way and took me from nowhere
to somewhere.

You and I will leave a trail. I shall
relive the event by telling myself
this exciting tale. I will read and
reread it to get thrilled on a
wintry night.

How else do you think will I
survive and warm the cockles
of my heart when you are gone?
Did I say when you are gone?
Oh, no! Don't ever go. Never
leave me.

XII

With a Bang

I resume the narrative. They are all impatient. Their appetite is whetted. They want to know us and what went on between us. They have seen the film *It Happened One Night.*

You think the experience is sacred and not for retailing. But our tale needs telling and retelling. It is an interesting story of a reluctant maiden who discovers desire and rebels against herself.

On public demand, I highlight
the climax. Say it in six words:
That was the night that was!

That glorious night, the radio is
turned on and its dire warning
turns you on. You start heavy
breathing. You stir and do what
you never did before.

Had wanted to but every time
you turned back.

You always saw me as a stranger.
Comes the night when a stranger
turns into self and the self turns
into a stranger!

The radio voice warns about
death coming after us from a
distant land. You look scared
and switch off the light.

We both plunge into darkness.
Outer light goes out. There is
dazzling darkness. We see the
dark of darkness. Darkness visible!

A different darkness that illumines
your fragrant body and I glimpse

heaven. We disappear in darkness.
We grope in inner light, feel each
other and find ourselves.

You gesture. I sense it in the dark.
I smell you in the dark. I breathe
your breath. Get closer and closer
till we merge. Words struggle to
come out. You say nothing. I say
nothing. We say nothing. Lips get
sealed. Bodies speak each to each.
The essential you emerges and greets
me with ecstasy. I reciprocate.

Then comes the moment, not gliding
like the bride but abruptly, without
notice, without music, without an
introductory remark, an endearing
couplet or a kiss.

Your skin gets feverish. It pulsates.
Its touch quickens my fingers dancing
on the drums. Our hearts are joined.
You can't wait. No time to say Yes.
Taken as said.

You lunge. In one fell swoop, fall over
me. Like a hungry lioness, you grab me,
drag me by force! Centuries of caution

end as you pull me and push me into
the dreamland.

The dam bursts with a roar. You rise
and fall, appear, disappear. You are not
you and there isn't any me anymore!

Your hair is ruffled, the cry is muffled.
the sigh is muffled. We pant, we moan.
Sleeping despair wakes up as Bliss. In a
flash, you are flesh and blood, a woman
of action. That moment of liberation
transforms you into a person.

The knife plunges. Emerges blood-washed,
having mined from the depth, a poem.
Lockdown Lyric! It flaunts the poem as
a precious booty from a bloody war.

I tear through the defenses, piercing
the veil of words. Does it call for a
victory parade? Eyes shut; we celebrate.
In your moist eyes, I see gratitude.
Hear a prayer. The curse of indecision
is lifted.

We have done it! It is not a sin in our
tradition. Fake Hindus have turned
love into an ugly word by clubbing
it with jihad.

You ignored them. Never checked my
religion before getting familiar with me.
You know now. My religion did not
matter to you.

They read your protest poems, kept an
eye on me and checked out my religion.

They cannot bear to see love. Hide love
to protect it from the hate-mongers
chasing lovers in deserted monuments,
remote parks, on lonely lanes, unlit
roads and in dim-lit cafes.

I describe our intimate encounter very
gingerly because I cannot risk assault
or murder by a vigilante mob or the
police. I have to presume that we live
in Pakistan.

Some misinterpret us. They see us
not in your room but in a historical
Garden. There is no apple tree here,
still they read ours as a tale of
The Fall. They want to witness and
enjoy a catastrophe and consequential
punishment.

We are not the couple they imagine.
Not engaged in mutual accusation.

We are bare without shame. Feel no guilt, no remorse. We do not need redemption and rehabilitation. They got misguided since you injected the theme of the forbidden in our story.

Be a fictive Eve. Celebrate *felix culpa*, the fortunate fall. We cannot hail the Son of God in this post-Christian world.

Critics will use the backdrop of the Pandemic to make their comments topical. They will cite Covid research.

Future historians will doubt that love was possible in 2021. They would not believe that I sang a Love Song in the year of great disaster when India was struck by the mighty combined force of dense mental pollution, polarisation, populism and the pandemic.

These are dark times indeed. But even the World War could not destroy love. Separation, tension and fear fuelled passion, killing propriety and decency. Love kept going with sirens and bombs. During the nights of blackouts, and air raids and days of rationing, love was

conducted in homes, shops, pubs,
lanes and in the red phone booths.

Homes turned into war trenches that
witnessed vigorous action of another
kind, echoing the slogan: *Make Love,
not War!*

War spawned numerous love children,
in defiance of nationalism. Women
sacrificed their all to strengthen the
trans-Atlantic special relationship.
A healthy hybrid evolved. American
body and British brain!

Is it perfume from your dress?
I tend to digress.

It was during the War that Eliot
published a love song that won
fame. It ushered the age of literary
modernism.

Today no bombers are raiding and no
bullets flying. No soldiers but farmers
are dying. The war-time spirit of
sacrifice is missing. We are driven by
envy and hatred. An insidious conflict
pushing civilians to a war.

Love is needed today. We have
a noble mission to love madly,
actually, and set an example in
a time of hate. Our tentative
phase has ended.

We have learnt to love. Desire
triumphed over hesitation and
dread. Platonic love discarded.
The Age of Prudence ended.

We have seen blood. Now on,
the moments of your new
liberation will become routine.

You enjoyed the rehearsal. Doing
it again would be easier and more
fun. Let us re-enact the awful daring
of that moment's surrender.
You found me. I found the real you.

Can we do it again and again? Are you
regretting the lost time?

Let us ensure that my ardour does
not flicker or fade and you do not
have second thoughts. Don't let me
examine my head, detect a bald
patch and feel old.

Hurry up! Hurry up, it is time.
They are coming to declare our
liaison illegal for reasons of caste
or creed or for no reason at all.

I shall not be afraid. Having tasted
it by chance, I shall eat the peach,
night after night. You have said Yes.
Why do you then give that enigmatic
smile? Give a free rein to your limbs
and imagination and let yourself go.
Say Yes once more with feeling!

A century made a big difference.
Prufrock and I parted company.
Prufrock left frustrated. I heard
her singing for me. Momentarily
fulfilled.

Our finale foxes critics who had
presumed I would end up like my
twin Prufrock. They were sure
that I, failure personified, would
end up like Prufrock.

Now they will advance an erudite
argument. They will say that my
triumph makes my song end on
a false note.

I did nothing. I do nothing. I was
always unsure. I had lost all hope.
It just happened one night. Critics,
not I, see it as my triumph.

KAK'S EUPHORIA ENDS!

XIII

What Next?

If it was a triumph, it came due to an
 event. I did nothing. I can do nothing.
 I am nothing.

You forced the moment to its crisis.
 and our union upon us. You turned
 mystical into physical. It took a crisis
 to resolve the crisis in our love.

Let me recall. You kept me waiting,
 night after night. What you gave,
 gave with such supple confusions
 that the giving famished the craving.

I was an actor in a non-action play,
 waiting for your arrival and my

salvation. I was alone, you were not
with me. Always mysteriously absent.

You never promised imminent
arrival, still I kept waiting, like
those two characters. I kept
waiting. Waiting for non-arrival.

Nothing happened. Nothing
happened till the night, a radio
voice woke you up and drowned
us in the life-nurturing sea of lust.

Super Flu that came threatening
to wipe out humanity cured you
of hesitation. It made you join me.
Turned a solo into a duet.

Covid saved me. Saved us! You never
said so but your eyes said it all. The
virus gave a twist to our tale. It led
to our fall for which I prayed for
long but of which I had lost hope.
Covid came and in our special case,
killed distance and healed.

It made our last act poignant, a
dazzling finale. The curtain fell,
not with a whimper but with a

bang. We made a grand exit
amid shouts of Bravo! Bravo!

I and Prufrock went different ways.
I was saved from the tragic end like
his. Released from a lonely existence.
The mermaids sang to me.

That momentous night you abruptly
assumed a new form, relenting at the
last moment, just before hugs and
handshakes were banned!

Before they threatened to barge
into the room to measure our body
heat and the distance dividing us.

Having missed the Swinging Sixties
and the song and dance, we lived a
dull life. Then that holy night, our
minds and bodies for the first time
danced in unison for a while before
being struck inert by paralysis of a
new kind.

Such a long journey it was. In the
end, my destiny changed and
I entered a new world. This is our
tale as told by me. I am no idiot,

nor meant to be. Our story will be called *Love in the Time of Covid.*

A global bestseller it will be though because of your eternal hesitation, it is devoid of heaving bodices and seething passion. Readers have to wait for its sequel that will have lust oozing out of every page! The book of mystery and miracle, a tale in which disease cures two love-sick souls! My great moment will leave a memento.

In this inspiring tale, you saved me. We made it in the nick of time. I got transformed by an external event.

I breathed a sigh of great relief and said all is well that ends well. But as it turned out, that was no end.

We were torn asunder after being given a taste of togetherness. Covid gave. Covid took it away. History took another turn.

After the exhilarating event, my transformed self went flying in the morning train. But at home, I saw the harsh daylight of the new Age. This Age dawned suddenly while I was overwhelmed by an event.

I celebrated my getting away from Prufrock's fate just because of an eventful night. Euphoria was not called for, in view of what followed.

I dread to imagine what could have happened to me. Had I left early last night, I would have been locked out without you. It would have been all over, with Covid killing me and my dream.

But the last night was as ephemeral as a passing train. In this Age of disruptive social distancing, quarantined bodies are jailed in tiny, sealed pods.
We are in a world upended by Covid. Do Not Touch, it has ordered. Not touch! Not feel! So heartless, so cruel! Nothing can heal us if that is denied.

Hugs prevent colds. Touch produces Happy Hormones. Your touch brought my neurotransmitters to life. Touch is

the sense crucial to human survival.
Without human connection, we perish.

Remember the last touch? Don't you
cherish it? Will you cherish it? I should
not ask you lest critics say that
I am always doubt-stricken.

In the new world, most lost intimacy
and let their mind space be crowded
with hundreds of virtual friends who
were unknown till yesterday.

Married couples sleep in separate rooms,
hide their faces behind masks and hug
by proxy provided by tiny yellow faces.
Old friends, if they happen to see each
other, smile from a distance and do not
embrace or shake hands.

We kiss from our sealed pods via
Zoom or Choom. All afflicted by
the passive numbness that afflicts
this blessed New Age.

Economists dominate post-pandemic
discourse on the hospitality and travel
businesses hit hard by social distancing.
Feelings have no market and of no
interest to share-holders.

The new world in which lovers face extinction gives fresh opportunities to others. Digital dating companies spread their wings. Architects design offices, schools, and factories with distant seating plans.

Futurists explain how businesses will benefit from a sharp decline in the numbers of those needing office space to work. They talk of remote workers. No thought given to remote lovers! Artificial Lover is arriving!

Businesses will promote online dating and algorithmic matching! That will validate traditional arranged marriages and crush the thrill of invention, creativity, chance and adventure and all that characterizes love.

We are virtual now. Cannot get real. Togetherness is not real. How do we cope with corporeal absence, sensory deprivation and collective anxiety?

Action gives authenticity to self.
Self cannot exist without sensation.
Physical solidarity is dead. Buried
under Tik Tok and Twitter. All
time is ScreenTime, DownTime,
FaceTime, TVTime, ZoomTime,
DoomTime!

We doom scroll and watch live
the end of imagination.

If we do distant chatting, my
modem may malfunction and we
shall be interrupted. If my Mute
button gets switched on, my lips
will move and say nothing!

If the virtual you feels like talking
to me, my broadband may lack
width or I will be lost among
chaotic updates and passwords
that will make you inaccessible
or turn me into an *Error.*

If my gadget plays mischief and
a filter makes me appear as the
Devil incarnate, you will get
Frightened. What a charade it
will be! I am daunted by the "ifs".

You may appear on my screen on Sundays but I will hate to have parasocial relationship instead of being with you in the same room night after night. It may not even be you. I may be approached by a digital clone with a morphed face.

In this Age, strangers will become real and real strange! Lovers and the idea of Love will be crushed by Artificial Intelligence and digital technology. Artificial Lover with synthetic consciousness and recorded monologue will lurk around, offering you relationship and remote intimate love.

Dangers abound. You may fall for a rogue serial Digital Dater! Computer-heart interface will follow computer-brain interface.

Start-Ups will start services for Digital Creatures. He will press a button and shout: "A Red Kiss. POD. ID 990." and get the set response: "Your order will be fulfilled in 10 seconds."

And to test the authenticity of my
love for you, you will use the
App based on the mind-reading
and heart-reading technology.

My love for you will be measured
by algorithms. Machine gaze may
disqualify me. Seeing my low love
score, you will distrust a human.

What will I do as a remote lover?
One can teach and learn online
but how does one love online?
The very meaning of love will be
altered in the New Age. It will
drain love of all meaning. Love
will not be the same.

Oh, for the nights when I could
walk to your flat and knock!
Connecting from afar was not
my dream.

I will be lonesome tonight. You
will not be with me for many
nights to come. How long will
you be away?

Uncertain times! Present messed
up by the past as well as an intruding

future. Present will run on and on. Will present ever pass? How will I live on the memory of our last ride and the last night together? How will I survive?

'Distant intimacy!' What is it, a lover asks. Two words yoked together to fool lovers. 'Distant intimacy' is anti-thesis of life.

Love needs an intimate contact. Extratemporal communion is not what I fancy. Getting into your inbox at night from afar will do me no good.

A new tribe of remote relationship managers will come up. Pop poets, psychologists, artists, cartoonists and comedians will be inspired by 'distant intimacy' to produce a new kind of work.

Self-help books will sell well. *How to process Love in the Post-Pandemic World?* will be the top best-seller.

I cannot process emotions on my own.
The guides on how to express love on
Zoom or Instagram are useless.

And you? Even if you take to the
new Digital life, you may soon be
hit by Zoom fatigue!

We are forced to stay apart in the
Age when we need each other most.
My sense of gloom and doom got
more intense this morning.

I am all set to abandon Hope and
Hope is waiting to abandon me.

What more is to come? I shudder
to think. Our relationship cannot
survive, with physicality bled out
of it.

Should I be grateful for what
I got one night? Are you? Do
you feel affected by trauma or
are you more resilient?

I worry that you are not worried.
You have restarted talking about
the dead and the dying and the
Government that keeps lying.

If a revolution disrupts this phase
and the political theatre ends,
you will pick up some other
noble cause to write poems on.

Your revolutionary spirit attracted
me and I began to sing in praise of
intellectual beauty. I loved the idea
of your being a poet-activist.

The romantic-progressive poet,
Amrita Pritam, illustrates how
romance and revolution are linked.
As a critic says, political idealism
is called romantic for a reason. Like
intimate romance, it also imagines
the crossing of borders on the basis
of passion into an unknown, with new
companions to forge a new world,
a new life and a new self.

You will continue to dream of
poetic love that must never be
shattered by a body awakened.
It was by chance that you stooped
to the common act of love.

You will be otherwise preoccupied.
You may again become your former
hesitant self. And from now on

there will be no K. Anand Kak
waiting patiently for you for long.

You will get over us. What will
happen to me? Detached from
you, I will be pushed into
isolation and depression.

I am human. I cannot bear very
much reality. I dread fate worse
than death. Mermaids will not
sing for me again. Mermaids
will never sing for me.

I crave for connection and touch.
But now I can speak to you only
in a voice mediated by technology.
Disembodied voice will make no
sense to me or to you. It will cause
cognitive dissonance.

I will be unable to write a single
word. My pen will lie lifeless without
your presence that awakened it every
night, and illumined Love.
My memory will dwell through
a love gone. In the sea of memories,
we will drown.

I can't go on, I'll have to go on.
Where I'll be, I do not know.

Is it the end of the story or
another beginning in store for
you and me, only future will tell.

I believe we would keep the
meaning of Love alive. There
is this virus that after having
saved us, will kill us. What
will survive of us is Love!

PRUFROCK & KAK

What a difference a century made!

A century ago, J. Alfred Prufrock was spared the numbness that would have silenced him and aborted his Love Song. It would have devastated him more than the silence of the mermaids. Prufrock escaped the virtual reality and an Artificial Lover. T. S. Eliot, his creator, did not live on to experience the horrors of this post-modern age. Eliot did not linger on to watch his unreal city transmuted into a dystopian space envisioned in laboratories by the VR and AR techies who conjured up a real unreal city! K. Anand Kak, as handicapped as Prufrock and as keen to love and be loved as Prufrock, faces more than just a reluctant maiden.

www.ingramcontent.com/pod-product-compliance
Lightning Source LLC
LaVergne TN
LVHW091324150826
845673LV00006B/1756